Qualitative Social Research

This text provides an easy-to-read introduction to qualitative research methods in social work, taking into account contemporary contexts and social conditions.

Drawing from a range of social work perspectives, it allows the reader to make the connection between social work values, theory and specific research methods and approaches.

Comprised of 11 chapters, it covers overarching epistemological perspectives and knowledge construction; designing a research question; research design and methods; data collection and analysis; research ethics and dissemination; and impact and research translation. Highlighting social work's unique commitment to social justice, it positions social work research as embedded in the profession's values.

As the first book to comprehensively connect social work values and emancipatory frameworks, including decolonising practices, with research methods, it shows readers the connection between social work theory and choices in relation to ethical research design.

This book is suitable for use on all BSW and MSW research modules across Australia and New Zealand as well as social work courses across the UK.

Priscilla Dunk-West is associate professor of social work at Deakin University. She has taught social work in Australia and England for many years, and her research interests include intimate relationships, families, sexuality and parenting.

Kate Saxton is chair of Pacific Communities of Practice and works as a senior lecturer in social work at the University of Southern Queensland. Kate's research interests include critical social work, intersectional feminism and decolonisation within education, research and practice.

Qualitative Social Research

Critical Methods for Social Change

Priscilla Dunk-West and Kate Saxton

Routledge
Taylor & Francis Group

LONDON AND NEW YORK

Designed cover image: Getty Image No. 1298834196

First published 2024
by Routledge
4 Park Square, Milton Park, Abingdon, Oxon OX14 4RN

and by Routledge
605 Third Avenue, New York, NY 10158

Routledge is an imprint of the Taylor & Francis Group, an informa business

© 2024 **Priscilla Dunk-West and Kate Saxton**

British Library Cataloguing-in-Publication Data
A catalogue record for this book is available from the British Library

Library of Congress Cataloging-in-Publication Data
Names: Dunk-West, Priscilla, author. | Saxton, Kate, author.
Title: Qualitative social research : critical methods for social change /
   Priscilla Dunk-West and Kate Saxton.
Description: 1 edition. | New York, NY : Routledge, 2024.
Identifiers: LCCN 2023058538 (print) | LCCN 2023058539 (ebook) |
   ISBN 9781032327891 (hardback) | ISBN 9781032327891 (paperback) |
   ISBN 9781003316732 (ebook)
Subjects: LCSH: Social sciences—Research—Methodology. |
   Critical thinking. | Social change.
Classification: LCC H62 .D7964 2024 (print) | LCC H62 (ebook) |
   DDC 300.721—dc23/eng/20240105
LC record available at https://lccn.loc.gov/2023058538
LC ebook record available at https://lccn.loc.gov/2023058539

ISBN: 978-1-032-32789-1 (hbk)
ISBN: 978-1-032-32759-4 (pbk)
ISBN: 978-1-003-31673-2 (ebk)

DOI: 10.4324/9781003316732

Typeset in Sabon
by Apex CoVantage, LLC

This book came about through teaching research methods, across continents and over a number of years, to social work students. Thank you to all of those students over the years for teaching me how to be a better teacher and trusting me with the task of demystifying social research. We wrote this book for all the future social work students out there who want to better connect their values and ethics and desire for positive social change with research. Thanks to my fabulous co-author, Kate: you're an inspiring and wonderful human, and it's been a pleasure working with you.

To Sam: I love doing life with you. Thank you for listening to me talk about this book ad infinitum. To my children Paxton and Blake: you're both the best.

Priscilla Dunk-West

This book is dedicated to my mum, who instilled in me a love of learning and always supported my pursuit of knowledge. I stand on the shoulders of giants, and I hope that this book serves to pave the way for the next generation of students who strive for social and ecological justice.

To Priscilla: Thank you for being a mentor, a listener, a coach, a comrade, a role model and most importantly, a friend. Your patience, kindness and authenticity are inspiring. To my son, Colin: you may never know how much you mean to me, but I hope that I can contribute to creating the type of world that honours and nurtures your beautiful soul. To Matt: thank you for the encouragement to 'just keep swimming', folding the never-ending loads of washing and for always believing in me.

Kate Saxton

Contents

Figures

About the Authors

Priscilla Dunk-West lives and works in Naarm (Melbourne) and is the author of the bestselling text *How to Be a Social Worker: A Critical Guide for Students*, co-author with Fiona Verity of *Sociological Social Work* and *Practising Social Work Sociologically: A Theoretical Approach for New Times*. She is co-editor with Trish Hafford-Letchfield of *Sexual Identities and Sexuality in Social Work: Research and Reflections from Women in the Field* and *Sexuality, Sexual and Gender Identities and Intimacy Research in Social Work and Social Care*. She has taught social work in Australia and England for many years, and her research interests include intimate relationships, families, sexuality and parenting. Priscilla is associate professor of social work at Deakin University.

Kate Saxton was born on Wadawarrung (also Wathaurong, Wathaurung) Country to a Dutch mother and American father of Irish and Cherokee ancestry. She is an award-winning educator and has taught both in Australia and across the Pacific Islands. She has written in the social work text *Pacific Social Work: Navigating Practice, Policy and Research*, and authored *Recontextualising Social Work in a Globalized World: Lessons from the Pacific*. Kate serves on the editorial board for the *Advances in Social Work and Welfare Education* journal and also serves as a committee member for the Women's Community Aid Association (WCAA) in Meanjin (Brisbane). She is chair of Pacific Communities of Practice and works as a senior lecturer in social work at the University of Southern Queensland. Kate's research interests include critical social work, intersectional feminism and decolonisation within education, research and practice. She lives in Meanjin with her partner, Matt, her son, Colin, and her Neapolitan mastiff, Arnold.

1   What Is Social Research?

Chapter Summary

- Social research has an important role to play in effecting positive social change.
- The contexts in which social research takes place are crucial to consider.
- Researchers ought to reflexively engage with their own positions as researchers.
- Broadly speaking, the purpose of social research can be to explore, explain, evaluate and encourage change.
- This textbook is arranged through chapters that explore the research process from its inception to its conclusion.

Introduction

In this chapter we discuss the foundations for this textbook. While there are many research books that describe the mechanics of research processes we believe that research can be a powerful tool for positive social change. This requires social research to be seen in its social, historical, political and cultural contexts. Throughout the book we note the ways in which these contexts ought to be taken into account in the shaping of research: from its inception to its conclusion. This chapter begins this work by examining what social research involves and how it fits within a social justice framework. We begin the chapter by prompting you, the reader, to think about what social research might mean, and then we explore the ways in which a social justice lens can assist us to make decisions about research design that upholds the values to which social work is attached.

Social Research

Let's begin by thinking about what we mean by the term 'social research'. The answer to the question: 'what is social research?' is seemingly straightforward. We think this introductory summary provides a succinct overview:

> social research is a purposive and rigorous investigation that aims to generate new knowledge. It is the intellectual tool of social scientists, which allows them to enter contexts of personal and/or public interest that are unknown to them, and to search for answers to their questions. Social research is about discovery, expanding the horizons of the known, of confidence, new ideas and new conclusions about all aspects of life.
>
> (Sarantakos, 2013, p. 4)

DOI: 10.4324/9781003316732-1

We invite you to read the quote a few times. What do you notice? What do you think are the main messages? To begin to think about social research, the final line from the quote tells us that social research is about 'all aspects of life'. In this sense, social research is related to society, individuals and all the groups and communities that are associated with the experience of being human. What about other species? Increasingly, social research is also recognising the importance of companion animals to humans' lives: this would also be included as an example of social research because it looks at the role that animals play in humans' lives (and vice versa). Here, we can begin to appreciate what it means to be human – to interact with others, to experience life, to be a part of societies, communities and groups. All of these aspects of being human are related to social research. In the first line of the quote, we see the word 'purposive' and that social research generates new knowledge. As we discuss further in Chapter 4, social research needs to contribute to knowledge about a particular issue; otherwise, the research could be considered unethical in that it places an unnecessary burden on participants for no particular benefit. This tells us that for social research to be carried out, we must not already know what we will find. There are many types of social research (see, for example, Sarantakos, 2013); however, for an introductory look at social research, we can group its purposes into three areas. Social research helps us to explore, explain and evaluate, which we will now discuss.

Social Research to Explore

Curiosity is a key driver in humankind's efforts to grow and develop knowledge, and we argue that a sociological imagination (Mills, 1959) is central to this aim. Social researchers are in a perfect position as 'insiders' to their social worlds. Drawing on curiosity about the world in which we live helps us to think about what we know about our worlds – our behaviours, attitudes and experiences – and to think about what this means for research. Exploratory research seeks to better understand that which is unknown or of which little is known about a particular topic. When you undertake a literature review (see Chapter 5), part of your goal is to identify what is known and what is lacking in understanding about a key topic so that you can position your research as aiming to address a 'gap' in knowledge. When you conduct your literature review and find limited information, this is often an indicator that further research is warranted in this field (Leavy, 2022).

Social Research to Explain

Research also helps us understand ourselves and explain phenomena. This type of research seeks to answer 'why' questions about certain social issues and phenomena. For example, why are some members of a community more impacted by a new social policy than others? Why are there connections between race, education and economic security? Why do certain groups hold particular beliefs regarding climate change or vaccinations or immigration? It is important to be mindful, however, that any research that attempts to definitively explain or assert a finding as 'factual' needs to be interrogated. All research is created and conducted within a context (more of this in Chapter 2) and needs to be understood and interpreted as representing an idea of 'truth' that has been generated within a specific socio-cultural and historical point of time. Correlation and causation research is often aligned with quantitative methods that aim to count, assess and measure social issues in numerical terms. Conversely, social research actively seeks to find answers to social issues that impact our world and better understand it because of it. It is worth pointing out that our research is only ever as impactful as the meaning we, as humans, ascribe to it.

Social Research to Evaluate

Social research can also help us understand what people think about a particular programme or service such as a social work service. A social worker may think that they are delivering an outstanding service, but without knowing what participants think about the service and asking for their experience of the service, the social worker won't know whether what they are doing is effective. When we want to understand the effectiveness of a programme or get a sense of the impact a policy has made in the lives of individuals and/or the community, evaluative research is a useful tool (Patton, 2015). In this sense, evaluation research is interested in whether the aims of a particular programme or policy have met their intended outcomes.

Social Justice and Power

In analysing the role of social theory, Steven Seidman notes the hope that early sociologists had in changing the world for the better – and the promise that social theory can and does offer positive social change in the present day (Seidman, 2016).

In this text, we seek to position social research within a critical framework as well as anchor our understanding of social research within a social justice lens. We discuss this in more detail in the following chapters; however, in order to have a strong foundation upon which to understand social research from a critical perspective, we need to explore what we mean by being 'critical' and what is also meant by 'social justice'. Since both of these concepts are central to social work, we argue that social research undertaken by social workers must bring about positive change. We position social research by social workers as being able to facilitate shifts in understanding, amplify the voices of those who have been historically silenced and a range of other positive outcomes, which we explore throughout this text. Let's now think about the connections between individual experiences and social conditions by undertaking exercises in critical thinking.

Critical Perspectives in Social Research

On the face of it, it doesn't seem controversial to assume that in a society, everyone ought to be happy. Or at least have the right to be happy. Let's think about what that might mean. Firstly, there will be diversity in terms of what happiness means to different people: one person's 'happy' might be another person's 'ecstatic'. Is one better than the other? What about people who are unhappy? Can we maintain happiness as a constant state? The ways that society narrates the idea of being happy are also wound up in these deliberations. The scholar Sarah Ahmed notes that historically, happiness has been used to justify the subjugation of people through colonisation and empire building (Ahmed, 2010). Ahmed also notes that the notion of happiness is embedded with dominant groups, to the detriment of minorities. Writing about the ways in which heterosexuality is represented in public life, she says:

> There is also no doubt that heterosexual happiness is overrepresented in public culture, often through an anxious repetition of threats and obstacles to its proper

achievement. Heterosexual love becomes about the possibility of a happy ending; about what life is aimed toward, as being what gives life direction or purpose, or as what drives a story. It is difficult to separate out narrative as such from the reproduction of happy heterosexuality.

(Ahmed, 2010, p. 90)

What do we learn about research in this brief look at the idea of happiness? As noted at the beginning of the chapter, in this book, we argue that social research ought to be placed in its social, historical, political and cultural contexts. Central to this aim is aligning the commitment to social justice and alignment with social work values alongside research design, execution and dissemination. When we think about social justice, we need to understand what we mean by this notion. In the example, we applied a universal lens with the following provocation: everyone ought to be happy. Yet once we begin to think about what we mean by happiness, how happiness has historically been used to justify colonial violence, we begin to use a critical lens, because we are taking into account how power is embedded and unequally experienced or *accessed* (to use a Foucauldian lens) in a society. Similarly, the representation of happiness Ahmed notes as being a part of the project of heterosexuality can be seen through popular culture: individual experiences are shaped by social conditions. When we think about social conditions in this context, Ahmed is noting the ways in which things such as stigma and discrimination are promoted through the absence of minority voices in popular culture. Social conditions are also important to noting patterns of inequality.

In social work education, we often ask students to reflect on their individual experiences and note the ways in which their values and views have been influenced by those around them. Thinking about power, inequality and lived experience involves the use of imagination when we ask social work students to be empathic to others to whom their own experience differs. We cannot unknow what we know by experiencing our biographies – and the use of imagination helps social work students to think outside of their own experiences to imagine challenges, joys and experiences of people with whom they may not be familiar (Dunk-West & Verity, 2018).

Let's now use another example to think about individual experience and social conditions. Imagine you think that societies ought to be just. Justice means that people in a society have equal access to resources, and no one is disadvantaged because of where they grow up, how much money they have or their identity (for example, their gender identity, their cultural identity and so on). The 'veil of ignorance' is a useful thought exercise authored by John Rawls, who suggests that we imagine that we are about to be born. For the purposes of this exercise, we can think about being about to be born as the 'original position'. Rawls explains this by noting:

[N]o one knows his [sic] place in society, his class position or social status; nor does he know his fortune in the distribution of natural assets and abilities, his intelligence and strength, and the like. Nor, again, does anyone know his conception of the good, the particulars of his rational plan of life, or even the special features of his psychology such as his aversion to risk or liability to optimism or pessimism. More than this, I assume that the parties do not know the particular circumstances of their own society. That is, they do not know its economic or political situation, or the level of civilization and culture it has been able to achieve. The persons in the original position have no information as to which generation they belong. These broader restrictions on knowledge are appropriate in part because questions of social justice arise between generations as well as within them. . .

(Rawls, 1999, p. 188)

Rawls asks us to imagine that there is a veil of ignorance relating to where we might be born, to which family or person, situation, society or institution. Reflecting on your own society, does it matter where a person is born, how much money they have or to whom they are related? Do these conditions affect people? If so, how? Is that just? The veil of ignorance as a thought experiment illuminates the ways in which our societies are unjust. This provides two things to the beginning researcher. First, it demonstrates the connections between individual experiences and social conditions, and second, it solidifies our commitment to a socially just world.

Through these thought exercises, we have begun to appreciate how social conditions shape individual experience. For research, this means that when we are conceptualising a research project, we need to use our critical thinking skills to think through our assumptions. We believe that this is a departure from research from other professions: the connections that we make through our theoretical and values to research are the central aim of this text. Social research therefore, needs to consider social conditions alongside the experiences of individuals, families, groups and communities.

Contextualising Social Work in Social Research

Although both authors of this text are social workers and social work educators, and we refer to social work throughout this text, we hope that other people interested in research will still find our text useful. There are many people who find themselves having to undertake research and who may want to have a critical perspective and a social justice lens: this book is for you also.

We also believe that research undertaken by social workers is a form of social work practice that is just as valid as working directly with people or working as a social work educator. Whereas social work is often seen as a practice involving working with people to affect positive change, research ought to also be a practice working to affect positive change.

Social work has its roots in understanding the ways in which social inequalities are experienced by individuals, groups, families and communities. In this sense, social work always casts a critical eye towards individual experiences and social conditions. This makes social work a unique profession: individual experiences are always shaped by the social conditions in which they take place. Understanding the ways in which social conditions shape our experiences, opportunities and access to resources involves drawing on sociological knowledge relating to power and patterns of inequality (Dunk-West & Verity, 2013).

As you work through this text, you will see that we agree that all research is influenced by the people who are carrying out the research. This acknowledgement comes from the traditions of feminist research (Letherby, 2003) and standpoint epistemology (Savolainen et al., 2023). Positionality statements are often included in social research in recognition of the role of the researcher in framing research problems. Positionality statements offer insights into researcher experiences, biographies and values. Some argue that these kinds of statements are "arbitrary, unnecessary and potentially harmful" (Savolainen et al., 2023, p. 1336); however, we take the view that our work cannot be separated from our experiences in the world and have therefore included our own positionality statements. We see this as a resistance to the ways in which knowledge has been sanitised or 'professionalised' (Maylea, 2021), for example, through the processes of colonialism (Yunkaporta, 2020).

About the Authors

Priscilla

I am a middle-aged woman, raised on Kaurna Country in the southern suburbs of Adelaide, South Australia. I grew up in social housing and come from a working-class background and am the first generation in my family to attend university. My father came from Bradford in England, and my mother is a white woman from European descent. I am also a queer disabled woman, a partner, mother, daughter, a sister and aunty, friend, ally and mentor. My work involves helping social work students to reflexively and critically engage with growing their social work identities. My research is shaped by all my experiences and identities, which intersect (Cho et al., 2013) and provide me with my worldview. I am a sociologist and social work academic who engages in research about sexualities, intimate relationships and family life.

Kate

I am a white-presenting cis-female, born on Wadawurrung Country in the area now known as Geelong. My maternal ancestry is Dutch, with my mother migrating to Australia after the Second World War. She was the first in her family to finish high school (and consequently went on to complete doctoral-level university studies). My paternal side is Native American (with traces of Irish and English thrown in for good measure). My paternal grandmother and great-grandmother were not allowed to talk about their Indigeneity, for this brought great shame on the family, and as fair-skinned people, they had married white with the vision of assimilation. These assimilation efforts did not preclude them from the experiences of poverty, classism, racism, substance misuse and violence, and my father, now in his 80s, was sent to live in an 'army camp' at age 2. My father talks very little of his family, and as children, we knew not to ask. As both my parents are immigrants, I am first-generation 'Australian', but I struggle to embody the sense of colonialist nationalism that comes with the Aussie label. Ironically, as a white, able-bodied, cis, heterosexual and middle-class woman, I struggle with the idea that this is where I 'belong'. I have always felt I belong in the margins and have always felt comfortable operating there despite being offered a place at the [white] table. I am passionate about social justice and have always felt a strong calling to 'make a change', which is how I stumbled upon social work in my 20s. Throughout my life, I have found solace in academia and research and efforts to 'meaning make'. I feel privileged when I get to walk alongside students on their own research journeys and meaning making.

Our Shared Perspective

As the authors of this text, we share our commitment to truth-telling about the history of social work in so-called Australia and borders beyond (see Bennett, 2021). As colleagues who teach and research in social work, we saw the need to create a text that sought to better theorise the connections between social work values and theory with research approaches. This text is the product of many years of teaching research and other subjects in social work, working with research higher-degree students and undertaking our own research.

Book Overview

We have written this book so that readers can dip in and out of chapters as it suits. Like other research textbooks, we have arranged the chapters so that the book can be read from beginning to end in the same way that a research project might be conceptualised, carried out and completed. We have included key ideas: theoretical and ethical ideas, for example, from social work and woven these into considerations for social research. This is a reflection on our approach to research that we are promoting: that research ought to be undertaken for positive change. Social justice, considerations of power and inequalities and social work values are intrinsic to such a project, and we step the reader through the ways in which social work research differs from other disciplines' research approaches.

In Chapter 2, we discuss epistemologies. This, we argue, is crucial to the social researcher because understanding one's epistemological stance means recognising one's worldview, values and understanding of knowledge. In Chapter 3, we examine the process of approaching a research area by looking at how to create a research question which successfully guides the research and draws from the insights gained in Chapter 2's discussion of epistemologies. Chapter 4 explores ethical considerations in social research, and like other chapters, this involves understanding our own values and those of the social work profession. One of the key tasks for a social researcher is to undertake a literature review, and in Chapter 5, we explore how to approach this task. In Chapter 6, we examine some of the major methodologies, and in Chapter 7, we outline the main ways that social research is undertaken through its methods. Chapter 8 looks at how to analyse data in social research. In Chapter 9, we step back to consider how we describe the findings in research. This involves understanding the ways in which we depict the people with whom we research. Chapter 10 outlines traditional and non-traditional dissemination methods and approaches, and the text concludes in Chapter 11.

Further Reading

Crotty, M. (2020). *Foundations of social research: Meaning and perspective in the research process.* Taylor & Francis Group.
Sarantakos, S. (2013). *Social research* (4th ed.). Palgrave Macmillan.

References

Ahmed, S. (2010). *The promise of happiness*. Duke University Press. https://doi.org/10.1515/9780822392781
Bennett, B. (2021). *Aboriginal fields of practice*. Bloomsbury Academic.
Cho, S., Crenshaw, K. W., & McCall, L. (2013). Toward a field of intersectionality studies: Theory, applications, and praxis. *Signs, 38*(4), 785–810. https://doi.org/10.1086/669608
Dunk-West, P., & Verity, F. (2013). *Sociological social work*. Ashgate.
Dunk-West, P., & Verity, F. (2018). *Practising social work sociologically: A theoretical approach for new times*. Palgrave.

Leavy, P. (2022). *Research design: Quantitative, qualitative, mixed methods, arts-based, and community-based participatory research approaches*. Guilford Publications.

Letherby, G. (2003). *Feminist research in theory and practice*. Open University Press.

Maylea, C. (2021). The end of social work. *The British Journal of Social Work*, *51*(2), 772–789. https://doi.org/10.1093/bjsw/bcaa203

Mills, C. W. (1959). *The sociological imagination*. Oxford University Press.

Patton, M. Q. (2015). *Qualitative research and evaluation methods* (4th ed.). Sage Publications.

Rawls, J. (1999). *A theory of justice* (Rev. ed.). Oxford University Press.

Sarantakos, S. (2013). *Social research* (4th ed.). Palgrave Macmillan.

Savolainen, J., Casey, P. J., McBrayer, J. P., & Schwerdtle, P. N. (2023). Positionality and its problems: Questioning the value of reflexivity statements in research. *Perspectives on Psychological Science*, *18*(6), 1331–1338. https://doi.org/10.1177/17456916221144988

Seidman, S. (2016). *Contested knowledge social theory today*. John Wiley & Sons, Incorporated.

Yunkaporta, T. (2020). *Sand talk how indigenous thinking can save the world*. Text Publishing Company.

2   The Social Construction of Knowledge

Chapter Summary

- Knowledge (what we know and how we know it) is constructed within a social, political, cultural, historical context.
- The study of what we know and how we know it is a field known as 'epistemology'.
- Your worldview and that of society around us informs what we consider to be the nature of reality as well as what is considered important or valuable.
- Certain voices and positions are privileged in the construction of knowledge, and as social workers, it is important to recognise the impact of positionality in the way in which knowledge is generated, promoted, celebrated, shared or ignored.
- All research contains bias. The role of the social worker researcher is not to be free from bias but rather to be aware of the ways that worldviews, values and beliefs interact to inform the way we engage with research activities.

Introduction

Research is an act of knowledge construction. You are contributing to what is known or not known about a certain topic, phenomenon or issue. In this chapter, epistemology, which is the study of knowledge, or how we know what we know, will be explored by using practical real-world examples. By unpacking research terms that have often been seen as daunting to new researchers, we will use plain language and practical examples to explore the ideas of ontology, epistemology and axiology. We will look at two dominant epistemological positions, social constructionism and positivism, and how these impact on the way we design, interpret and engage with the research process. We also highlight the risk of dominant discourse and research bias in subjugating diverse knowledge bases, including those of First Nations communities. By understanding the process of knowledge construction and knowledge consumption, we can begin to interrogate the voices and opinions that may (or may not) be privileged in the research process. We are then able to be cognisant of our own research positionality and understand the significance of critical reflection within social work research while appreciating the role critical reflection plays in assisting us to navigate epistemological tensions.

Research projects can also be considered political in the sense that they are primarily driven with outlining boundaries to distinguish between them and others and thus create a barrier between who's in and who's out. This chapter encourages social work researchers to be conscious of the intricate forces that shape knowledge and research practices and the role that critical reflection can play in demystifying these forces. Critical

DOI: 10.4324/9781003316732-2

reflection as a distinct skill set for both research and practice is examined, along with the tools that students and practitioners can employ to think sociologically and historically about 'whose voice' has dominated knowledge acquisition, theory development and empirical work. This chapter will show the reader how to think critically about research and how to approach particular fields of study in a way that aligns with both the social research topic under investigation and the overarching values of social work. By embracing critical reflection and being aware of their own biases and positionality, researchers can contribute to more meaningful and impactful research that aligns with the values of social work and promotes positive social change.

What Is Knowledge?

Have you ever wondered, how do I know what I know? Or why do I believe what I believe? Or even still, why do I think how I think? Chances are these processes are so automatic that you may not be aware that these processes have been learned and heavily influenced by the world around you. Sometimes, this learning has been deliberate or conscious, such as learning about the solar system in primary school, or how to read and write. Other times, this learning has been more subtle and socially conditioned, such as knowing to say "hello" when you meet someone or the way that some people 'know' that girls are more emotional than boys. Often, we take these for granted as facts and don't ask questions about how do I know this to be true. To add more complexity to the way we know, there are deliberate social, cultural, religious and political forces that attempt to control what we know and how we know and sometimes even what we are allowed to know (McAuliffe et al., 2023). Consider the example of studying research as part of a university degree: was this your choice, or did somebody else decide on your behalf that you needed to 'know' this information? Epistemology, which is a word clouded in much mystery and ambiguity, is quite simply the study of knowledge. When we study and examine what we constitute as knowledge, sometimes referred to as 'fact' or 'truth', we are engaging with the epistemological process (Crotty, 2020). Of course, everyone believes what they know to be right; that's the very reason we hold on so tightly to our views. It is also a big reason for debates, tensions and conflict in the broader social world and in research specifically. This chapter hopes that you will no longer take knowledge for granted and start to become aware of the intricate forces that shape the way we consume, construct and disseminate knowledge sources and research.

Epistemology, Ontology and Axiology

Epistemology is a term which refers to how we understand and gain knowledge about the world around us. It's all about how we come to know things and what we consider to be 'true' or reliable information (Crotty, 2020). In social work, epistemology is especially important because it helps us understand how knowledge is created and shaped within different social contexts. For example, the knowledge produced in a scientific laboratory may be different from the knowledge held by a religious community. Both forms of knowledge are shaped by different social, cultural and historical factors. Conflicts and tensions arise when certain groups position one set of knowledge beliefs as more reliable; that is, they consider their beliefs to be more true than those of other groups.

Social work practice, research and theory are influenced by a concept known as post-modernism. Post-modernism introduces the idea that there can be multiple truths or realities and that these are created through the words that we use, daily language and dominant discourses (Briskman et al., 2009). As such, social work recognises that knowledge is not just some objective truth that exists out there (Fook, 2023). It's actually influenced by our social experiences, cultural beliefs and the social structures we live in. Epistemology in social research helps us to understand the limitations and biases that can exist in knowledge production. It reminds us that our understanding of the world is not necessarily complete or neutral. Our social positions, such as our race, gender or class, can shape what we know and what we don't know (Walter, 2019). So studying epistemology in research helps us uncover these biases and strive for a more inclusive and accurate understanding of the world. It explores questions like: Who gets to decide what counts as knowledge? How is knowledge produced, validated and shared in society? And how does social power influence what we know and how we know it? Essentially, epistemology is all about exploring how we come to know things, recognising the social influences on knowledge and critically examining the way knowledge is created and shared in society.

Ontology is a concept that often comes up in discussions related to social work research. Ontology is a branch of philosophy that deals with understanding the nature of reality, existence and what things actually are (Walter, 2019). Whereas epistemology looks at *how* we come to view reality, or truth, epistemology considers *what is* truth. Because social work draws from sociological theories, an important aspect of ontological inquiry in social research is understanding how social reality is constructed and maintained (Sarantakos, 2017). It recognises that social phenomena are not fixed or immutable but can change over time (Crotty, 2020). For example, concepts like race, gender or identity are socially constructed, meaning they are shaped by society's ideas, norms and practices. Ontology helps us analyse how these social constructs come into being, how they are maintained and how they influence our understanding of the world.

An example of how ontological viewpoints apply in social work research and practice can be seen in the understanding of poverty. One ontological viewpoint might approach poverty as a purely individual-level issue, focusing on personal traits, choices and behaviours as the primary causes of poverty. This perspective may emphasise personal responsibility, self-determination and individual efforts to overcome poverty. It may argue that poverty is a result of individual shortcomings rather than structural or systemic factors. In contrast, another ontological viewpoint might view poverty as a social and systemic issue. This perspective recognises that poverty is not solely a result of individual actions but is influenced by broader social, economic and political factors. It acknowledges the impact of social structures, policies and unequal distribution of resources on poverty. This viewpoint emphasises the role of systemic barriers, such as discrimination, unequal access to education and healthcare and economic inequality in perpetuating poverty. These two ontological viewpoints present different understandings of poverty, with one focusing on individual-level causes and responsibilities while the other emphasises the systemic and structural aspects of poverty. These different perspectives shape how poverty is conceptualised, approached and addressed in terms of policies, interventions, research design, consumption and dissemination and social change initiatives. Your ontological position will depend on how you view the world and how you consequently develop your research questions and design.

Axiology is another concept of philosophy that is used in social research. Whereas ontology looks at the nature of reality, or 'truth', axiology considers what elements of reality we value or consider important (Killam, 2013). Axiology also intersects with ontology by influencing how we perceive and interpret reality (Crotty, 2020). Our values and ethical beliefs shape the lenses through which we view social phenomena, including poverty. They can influence our judgements about what needs to be addressed, how resources should be allocated and what social change initiatives should be pursued. In the context of social work and research, axiology plays a role in examining and assessing the values associated with different ontological viewpoints. For example, when discussing poverty, axiology comes into play in evaluating the moral or ethical implications of different perspectives. It involves considering questions such as: What values are being prioritised in each ontological viewpoint? How do these values shape our understanding and responses to social issues like poverty?

Axiology is closely connected to ontology in the sense that both branches explore fundamental aspects of human existence and understanding (Crotty, 2020). While ontology seeks to understand the nature of reality, axiology delves into the evaluation and understanding of what is valuable as well as what is considered morally 'right' or 'wrong'. Axiology provides a framework for critically examining the values underlying different ontological viewpoints as well as evaluating the ethical implications and considerations associated with our understanding of social issues. It helps us navigate the complex moral and evaluative dimensions inherent in discussions about social phenomena (Walter, 2019). Axiology is useful because it helps us to name bias in research and avoid assumptions that research can be neutral or apolitical. Not all disciplines share the same axiological or ontological viewpoints, and this can lead to differences in understanding both the nature and causes of social phenomena and how best to research and respond to them. This also leads to tensions in how research funding and resources are allocated and prioritised. An exploration of the most dominant ontological positions is explored in the next part of this chapter.

Social Constructionism

An influential epistemological view in social work theory, research and practice is that of social constructionism. A key tenet of social constructionist theory is a belief that reality is socially, culturally and historically constructed (Bloomberg & Volpe, 2012), and this allows for the possibility for multiple meanings or realities to co-exist (Bryant & Charmaz, 2010). This is in stark contrast to other epistemologies that would argue there can be only one objective, or absolute truth. Rather than claiming to be 'objective', constructionist approaches to research do not claim to be free from bias. Constructionist approaches emphasise the possibility for multiple realities, acknowledge the researcher participants' respective positions and values and concede that data is inherently partial. Indeed, social constructionism views inquiry as value bound rather than value free, implying that the process of research is inherently influenced by the views and role that the researcher plays in the process (Bloomberg & Volpe, 2012). The social constructionist researcher seeks to understand a certain reality or worldview by interacting with research participants within the cultural and historical settings they interact; they must recognise that their own personal worldviews shape their interpretations and thus attempt to position themselves within the research process by acknowledging that both researcher and participants construct meaning within the research process. Constructionist research acknowledges the subjective nature of reality and acknowledges that the researcher can do no more than interpret these realities in connection with their own beliefs and understandings of how the world is constructed.

Positivism

In contrast to constructionist paradigm, a positivist would argue that the researcher is a neutral observer, and thus, analysis need not take into account the role of the research participant and the conditions in which research is collected (Charmaz, 2017). Positivism draws from the natural sciences to test theories regarding phenomena, human kind and society. It promotes objectivity, imperialism and non-bias in an attempt to apply universal 'laws' or truths about the world (Liamputtong, 2010). In contrast to social constructionism, empiricism, which is the foundation of positivism, views reality as universal, objective and quantifiable and is from where the term 'empirical evidence' stems from in research. From this perspective, it is argued that reality is the same for you as it is for me, and through the application of science, we can identify and measure the world (Crotty, 2020). Positivism argues that the world is the way it is regardless of human consciousness (Sarantakos, 2017). Positivism is appealing because of its promise of objectivity and capacity to find one ultimate truth. For this reason, it is often viewed as a more reliable way of engaging in research (Crotty, 2020). However, that does not mean that one can simply ignore or fail to cast a critical eye over the complex way in which power shapes knowledge in varying contexts and environments. Too often, certain types of knowledge are privileged over others (Saxton, 2019). For this reason, social workers offer a unique contribution to research by highlighting the often-hidden assumptions and invisible privileges that occupy the research space.

Indigenous Epistemologies

Although dominant research discourses such as positivism and rationalism have played a significant role in the development of technology and biomedical advancements in recent years, the claims of objectivity fail to account for the role of humans within the research process; this includes both the research design and interpretation of results as well as what is considered valuable to research in the first place. This has meant that other ways of knowing, including Indigenous knowledge, have been discounted for lacking validity and reliability (Mafile'o et al., 2019). Fortunately, attitudes are beginning to shift, with a growing recognition of the ways in which Indigenous knowledges play, for example, in our response to climate change (Hill et al., 2020). While the importance and recognition of First Nations and subjugated knowledge have increased in recent years, this does not always carry as much perceived validity as the expert knowledge of scientists (Trevithick, 2011). Thus, Indigenous knowledge runs the risk of being discounted or considered less relevant (Ravulo, 2016). If social work researchers are to be authentic in their commitment to anti-oppressive practices, then research activities also need to ensure that certain voices are not marginalised in the process.

Research, in its most simplistic of definitions, can be viewed as a process of information seeking. Yet the term has come to symbolise a process largely symbolic of Western scientific 'enlightenment' (Ravulo, 2019). In fact, research has played an ongoing role in colonisation efforts and, at times, has been used to justify racial oppression and genocide. This history and a legacy of researching 'on' rather than 'with' communities is one barrier to engagement when developing research that impacts Indigenous communities (Mafile'o et al., 2019). The incongruence between Western ideological assumptions and the lived experiences of Indigenous communities is another factor that contributes to poorly translatable research. For research to be meaningful, it needs to be relevant and contextually appropriate to the communities it directly impacts. These considerations will be examined further in Chapter 10. Furthermore, if research is to avoid the risk of being neocolonial, researchers need to be aware of the ways in which knowledge is constructed and privileged (Saxton, 2019; Mafile'o et al., 2019). Being aware of these privileges and the cultural assumptions within research design is a vital first step in ensuring ethical and anti-oppressive research practices.

Researcher Bias and Positionality

Given the ease with which certain knowledges can be privileged over others during the research process, critical reflection is essential for social workers because it allows us to challenge biases, promote social justice, validate marginalised voices and engage in ethical and inclusive research practices (Saxton, 2021; Fook, 2023). By embracing critical reflection, social workers can enhance the quality and impact of their research, contributing to positive social transformation and a more equitable society. Critical reflection is a tool that helps us to navigate tensions in epistemology and ask crucial questions as to the nature of the research 'problem' or issue to be investigated, whose voices have been highlighted or silenced in the development of the research topic and whether subtle biases are indeed reinforcing disadvantage and forms of oppression. The summary that follows shows the ways in which critical reflection is used in research to examine our own research positionality and bias while simultaneously working to uphold the values inherent in ethical social work research.

The role of critical reflection in social research

Challenging assumptions and biases: Critical reflection allows social workers to examine their own assumptions, biases and preconceived notions that may influence their research process and findings. By recognising and addressing these biases, we as social researchers can strive for objectivity and a deeper understanding of the issues under investigation.

Promoting social justice and equity: Social work research often focuses on issues of social justice and equity. Critical reflection helps us identify power imbalances and social inequalities that may be perpetuated within the research process itself. By critically examining these dynamics, we can work towards conducting research that is more inclusive, respectful and empowering for all individuals involved.

Enhancing reflexivity: Critical reflection fosters reflexivity, enabling us to be aware of our positionality and the impact it has on the research. This self-awareness helps us understand how our background, experiences and social location may influence the research design, data collection and interpretation.

Validating the voices of marginalised groups: Social work research often involves working with vulnerable and marginalised populations. Critical reflection ensures that the voices and perspectives of these groups are not overshadowed or misinterpreted during the research process. It encourages social researchers to be sensitive to the cultural, social and historical contexts of the individuals and communities who participate in research.

Ethical considerations: Critical reflection prompts us to continuously evaluate the ethical dimensions of our research. It ensures that research is conducted with integrity, informed consent and respect for human rights. Ethical considerations should be at the forefront of the research process, and critical reflection helps us navigate potential ethical dilemmas effectively.

Creating social change: Social work is ultimately focused on creating positive social change and improving the lives of individuals and communities. Critical reflection helps to identify opportunities for advocacy, policy changes and actions that address the root causes of social issues.

Conclusion

This chapter delves into the concepts of epistemology, ontology and axiology, discussing their role in shaping how we understand and interpret reality. Social constructionism, with its recognition of multiple realities and subjectivity, challenges the notion of one absolute truth, while positivism strives for objectivity and thus claims to be universal in its application (regardless of the existence of diverse social and cultural contexts). Not all disciplines recognise that reality is socially constructed, and this is an area which can cause tension in both the ways in which research is designed and the nature of the social issue or phenomena under investigation. Given these tensions, this chapter has argued that research projects are inherently political, because they create boundaries that distinguish insiders from outsiders, shaping the knowledge production process. Understanding the construction and consumption of knowledge enables researchers to interrogate the privileged voices and opinions present in research and become cognisant of their own positionality in the research process.

This chapter also identifies the ways in which certain knowledges, or epistemologies, are subjugated in the research process. We have highlighted the importance of acknowledging and valuing Indigenous epistemologies, recognising the role of self in the construction of reality and the possibility for multiple realities, or belief systems, to coexist. We have also outlined the ways in which critical reflection can assist researchers to navigate epistemological questions and merge research goals with the values inherent in ethical social work practice. Critical reflection serves as a tool to navigate the complexities of epistemological tensions and encourage researchers to be aware of their own positionality and potential biases. By engaging in critical reflection, social workers can challenge assumptions, promote social justice, validate marginalised voices and conduct ethical and inclusive research. It empowers researchers to question the privileged knowledge sources and perspectives and strive for a more equitable and transformative research process. Overall, a critical awareness of our ontological position provides us a structured framework for understanding complex social phenomena and promoting effective research design, analysis and collaboration in social work.

Further Reading

Esposito, J., & Evans-Winters, V. (2021). *Introduction to intersectional qualitative research*. SAGE Publications Ltd.

Fook, J. (2023). *Social work: A critical approach to practice* (4th ed.). SAGE Publications Ltd.

Rawsthorne, M., Tseris, E., Howard, A., Terare, M., & Sharma, A. (2023). *Using social research for social justice: An introduction for social work and human services* (1st ed.). Routledge.

Tuhiwai Smith, L. (2021). *Decolonizing methodologies: Research and indigenous peoples* (3rd ed.). Bloomsbury.

Walter. M. (2019). *Chapter 1: The nature of social science research: Social research methods* (4th ed.). Oxford University Press.

References

Bloomberg, L., Dale., & Volpe, M. (2012). *Completing your qualitative dissertation: A roadmap from beginning to end* (2nd ed.). SAGE Publications.

Briskman, L., Pease, B., & Allan, J. (2009). Introducing critical theories for social work in a neo-liberal context. In B. Pease, J. Allan & L. Briskman (Eds.), *Critical social work: Theories and practices for a socially just world* (2nd ed., pp. 3–14). Taylor & Francis Group.

Bryant, A., & Charmaz, K. (2010). *The SAGE handbook of grounded theory*. SAGE Publications.

Charmaz, K. (2017). The power of constructivist grounded theory for critical inquiry. *Qualitative Inquiry, 23*(1), 34–45. https://doi.org/10.1177/1077800416657105

Crotty, M. (2020). *Foundations of social research: Meaning and perspective in the research process*. Taylor & Francis Group.

Fook, J. (2023). *Social work: A critical approach to practice* (4th ed.). SAGE Publications Ltd.

Hill, R., Walsh, F. J., Davies, J., Sparrow, A., Mooney, M., Wise, R. M., & Tengö, M. (2020). Knowledge co-production for Indigenous adaptation pathways: Transform post-colonial articulation complexes to empower local decision-making. *Global Environmental Change, 65,* 102161. https://doi.org/10.1016/j.gloenvcha.2020.102161

Killam, L. (2013). *Research terminology simplified: Paradigms, axiology, ontology, epistemology and methodology*. Laura Killam.

Liamputtong, P. (2010). *Performing qualitative cross-cultural research*. Cambridge University Press.

Mafile'o, T., Mataira, P., & Saxton, K. (2019). Towards a Pacific-indigenous research paradigm for Pacific social work. In J. Ravulo, T. Mafile'o & D. Bruce Yeates (Eds.), *Pacific social work: Navigating practice, policy and research* (1st ed.). Routledge. https://doi.org/10.4324/9781315144252

McAuliffe, D., Boddy, J., & Chenoweth, L. (2023). *The road to social work and human service practice*. Cengage AU.

Ravulo, J. (2016). Pacific epistemologies in professional social work practice, policy and research. *Asia Pacific Journal of Social Work and Development, 26*(4), 191–202. https://doi.org/10.1080/02185385.2016.1234970

Ravulo, J. (2019). Social work as a recognised profession in the Pacific region. *International Social Work, 62*(2), 712–725.

Sarantakos, S. (2017). *Social research*. Bloomsbury Publishing.

Saxton, K. (2019). Privileging participation in the Pacific: Researcher reflections. *Aotearoa New Zealand Social Work, 30*(4), 9–12. https://doi.org/10.11157/anzswj-vol30iss4id606

Saxton, K. (2021). Recontextualizing social work in a globalized world: Lessons From the Pacific. In *Practical and political approaches to recontextualizing social work* (pp. 192–208). IGI Global.

Trevithick, P. (2011). *Social work skills and knowledge: A practice handbook*. McGraw-Hill Education (UK).

Walter, M. (2019). The nature of social science research. In M. Walter (Ed.), *Social research methods* (4th ed., pp. 3–28). Oxford University Press.

3 Designing a Research Question

Chapter Summary

- Asking a research question is a powerful act, and social researchers need to be aware of their own biases and ethical standpoints.
- Before asking a research question, it is important to understand the history of research questions that have been asked about a particular topic.
- Positioning ethical considerations about the impact of research, the purpose of research and the contribution research might make are important to the narrowing down process.
- It is important to be realistic about the limited scope that research has and its place in the literature.
- Research questions are specific, and the purpose of research is to generate data that answers the research question.

Introduction

The design of a research question is not only a pragmatic task, it is an ethical and political one. Research questions provide a foundation for research projects and speak to the chosen epistemological orientation and values inherent to social work. Research questions are also embedded in time and space – in history and society: the questions we ask are reflected in the social and historical conditions in which we find ourselves. This chapter explores the complexities inherent to the asking of research questions and considers power in relation to this act of asking. In this chapter, we will also discuss the key ingredients that are vital to consider when constructing a research question. We begin by considering. . .

If you are asking a research question, it is likely that you will be a professional, have completed or be completing university studies. Why is this an important point to make? As discussed previously, it is important to recognise that, historically, those who asked research questions were in privileged positions. For example, if we think about what we know about mental health through research from past studies, it is likely that the research questions that were posed were asked by those *without* mental health diagnoses. This is because mental health has traditionally been defined by psychiatric discourses which separate the 'well' from the 'unwell' (Foucault, 2006). More recently, there has been a movement within mental health that argues for knowledge construction about mental health by people with lived experience of mental health issues and argues for a activism-led framework of 'madness' (Beresford, 2020). Why is this important, and what does it have to do with research? The regulation of mental health through biomedical discourses flows through to research, including the kinds of research questions being asked. Research questions (or testing an hypothesis) will be framed through a biomedical lens and might be connected to testing the efficacy of a certain drug to mitigate the effects of a mental health *disorder*. On the other

DOI: 10.4324/9781003316732-3

hand, research questions which emerge from people who have lived experienced mental health diagnoses may be more interested in better understanding the shared experiences of people with mental health diagnoses. This kind of research question might ask something such as: What are the experiences of older people diagnosed with depression accessing support through general practice health services in rural England?

Social work is interested in the ways in which power is expressed and utilized, and our commitment to social justice means that we are always looking for ways to challenge inequalities. Social work research must therefore always be aware of power and inequalities and work to reduce power imbalances in its research processes. Thinking about the example around mental health, we are therefore always cognisant of who is asking the research question and what claims they have to speak on behalf of others.

Social research has its own rules, language, theoretical perspectives and methods, which makes it, at times, impenetrable to people who have not studied these things. While researchers are now arguably more engaged with the translation of research to the public sphere through media activities and resource development, universities continue to consider the publication of research in peer-reviewed journals as the most important measure of esteem. We will discuss research dissemination in Chapter 10; however, it is important when framing research questions to think about to whom the research might matter and to whom the findings are important. Research that occurs within universities can suffer from a lack of exposure to the outside world, and the publication of research in a journal article, for example, will likely only be read by other academics. Similarly, academic conferences are somewhat 'closed spaces' in which academics tell other researchers about their research findings. This is particularly the case for medical conferences in which latest findings about a particular approach might be relayed to other medical practitioners who can enhance their practice as a result. Social work conferences are sometimes attended by practitioners or social workers in their fields of practice, yet why is it that conferences don't always include people with 'lived experience' of a particular phenomenon? All of these considerations become important when thinking about to whom the research findings ought to be communicated as well as at the very beginning of the research process when the researcher asks a research question. Let's think about power and how it is relevant to research. When framing a research question, taking into account the power that a researcher may have involves:

- Reducing 'impenetrable' language
- Thinking about one's audience: To whom is the research important, and how will you honour participants' experiences and voices?
- Whether your question has been asked before
- What is different about a social work lens in the framing of the research question?
- Whether you are reproducing inequalities, stigma or making other negative assumptions

Social Justice

Social work's commitment to social justice is relevant not only to social work practice but also to research. This includes the ways in which we frame research questions. The following statement from the International Federation of Social Workers (IFSW) outlines the ways in which both human rights and social justice are embedded in social work:

> The overarching principles of social work are respect for the inherent worth and dignity of human beings, doing no harm, respect for diversity and upholding human rights and social justice.

Yet what does it mean to 'do no harm' or 'respect diversity' in a research sense? What does the 'inherent worth and dignity of human beings' have to do with research? How can we apply our knowledge about social inequalities to social research? The answer to these questions is that social justice and human rights should be considered at the very beginning stage in research, from the time that the research question is being formulated, in order to avoid reproducing inequalities through research.

As members of societies, we are no more immune to the effects of bias, stigma and shame that any other person. Therefore, when we ask a research question, we need to employ our critical thinking skills to uncover our underlying assumptions about a particular issue. Let's explore what this means in practice.

Imagine that you are interested in single parenting. You might have an idea about a project that looks at the experiences of teenagers who are parented in a single-parent household in an urban Australian setting. It might seem reasonable to formulate a research question like:

What are the impacts on young people who are from a single-parent household living in Melbourne?

You might look at the available literature and note a number of articles that explore the impacts of divorce on children. You might find other research that looks at longer-term outcomes for people who come from single-parent households.

Let's think about some of the assumptions we are making in beginning to formulate a research question relating to a single-parent household. Notice that in the proposed research question we ask about the 'impacts' for young people who are in a single-parent household. Why would we use that term? What connections might there be to other research that looks at the 'impact' of parental divorce on children? Once we start to critically reflect on the term 'impact', we can begin to apply our critical lens to think through the social, cultural, historical and political dimensions to thinking about family life. Firstly, we might need to reflect upon our own experiences of being parented and whether biographical events are negatively influencing our research focus. The following prompts may help in such a process of critical thinking:

Do I agree or disagree with the following statements?

- Divorce is bad for children.
- Being in a dual-parent household is better for children.
- Children need male and female role models.
- I feel sorry for children with one parent.

These provocations are deliberately divisive but are designed for the researcher to reflect on their ideas about family life and, specifically, the ways in which research about single parenting might be approached. Part of reflecting is also about thinking about why you may think what you think. This involves thinking about society's values and attitudes towards particular people. Going back to our research question, we can further interrogate the term 'impacts'. In framing the research question with the term 'impacts' implies that there are inherent 'impacts' on a child which relate to single parenting and that these are negative. Further reflection might produce a different approach. For example, it may be that you are interested in the economic challenges for single parents or the connections that single parents have that assist them in raising their child/ren. Both of these areas of research will produce very different research questions. Yet how do you choose what area you are interested in pursuing? In the next section we move on to consider who is asking the research question before examining how to narrow down the research question.

Who Is Asking?

As we discussed at the beginning of the chapter, considering power is inherent to the focus and, indeed, the carrying out of research, and historically, privilege has accompanied the researcher alongside this process. Privilege relates to the position of the researcher as an expert with authority to make statements about particular communities, individuals and even populations. There is a growing movement which recognises the power that particular disciplines have had in speaking on behalf of people with lived experience of a particular phenomenon and which questions the ways in which stigma and shame and 'othering' are reified through doing so. At the beginning of this chapter, we considered the ways in which the medical professions have historically been the ones to define mental health and mental illness (Beresford, 2020). Another prominent example of the risk of research serving to further marginalise another group is research about lesbian, gay, bisexual, transgender and queer people (LGBTQ). It is useful to think historically about the population on which you intend to focus your research. LGBTQ research has developed in line with social theories about identity (Serrano Amaya & Ríos González, 2019), so looking back to early research around homosexuality promulgates the idea that sexual minorities are somehow abnormal and therefore deviant (Lenza, 2004).

Thinking about human rights can help us to understand if the position of the researcher in the context of the subject area and whether the research and researcher are a good fit. We discuss ethical research in detail in Chapter 4.

Narrowing Down

The process of narrowing down is an important step in formulating a research question. Most researchers will find themselves wanting to achieve a great deal through their research. Unfortunately, this is all too often an impossible task. The beginning researcher will often want to have more than one research question; however, this makes managing a small research project almost impossible.

When narrowing down the research question, knowing what research or knowledge exists is crucial. Undertaking a literature review, as discussed in Chapter 5, will help you organise the key areas of knowledge that relate to your research, which will also inform your research question.

Choices About Focus

Sometimes, difficult decisions need to me made about the scope of research, because the researcher can only ask a research question about a relatively narrow area of inquiry. It helps for some people to draw and map out what comes to mind with a particular topic. For example, if we take the term 'mental health', we can reflect on what we know about this area, think about how we know it and then what key debates, areas of practice, experiences of mental health and related issues are connected to mental health. We have begun this process in Figure 3.1.

Social Workers?

Role of "professionals"

Foucault

Role of history is it better now??

Cultural contexts

Young people

Institutions hospitals station settings

Mental health

"illness"

History DSM homosexuality

Social models of health

Lived experience

Psychiatry medicine categories?

Isolation? Connectedness

Mindfulness

Diagnosis treatment

Mad studies

Individuals/Society
– Cultural   – Dis/ability
– Social   – Class
– Age
– Gender

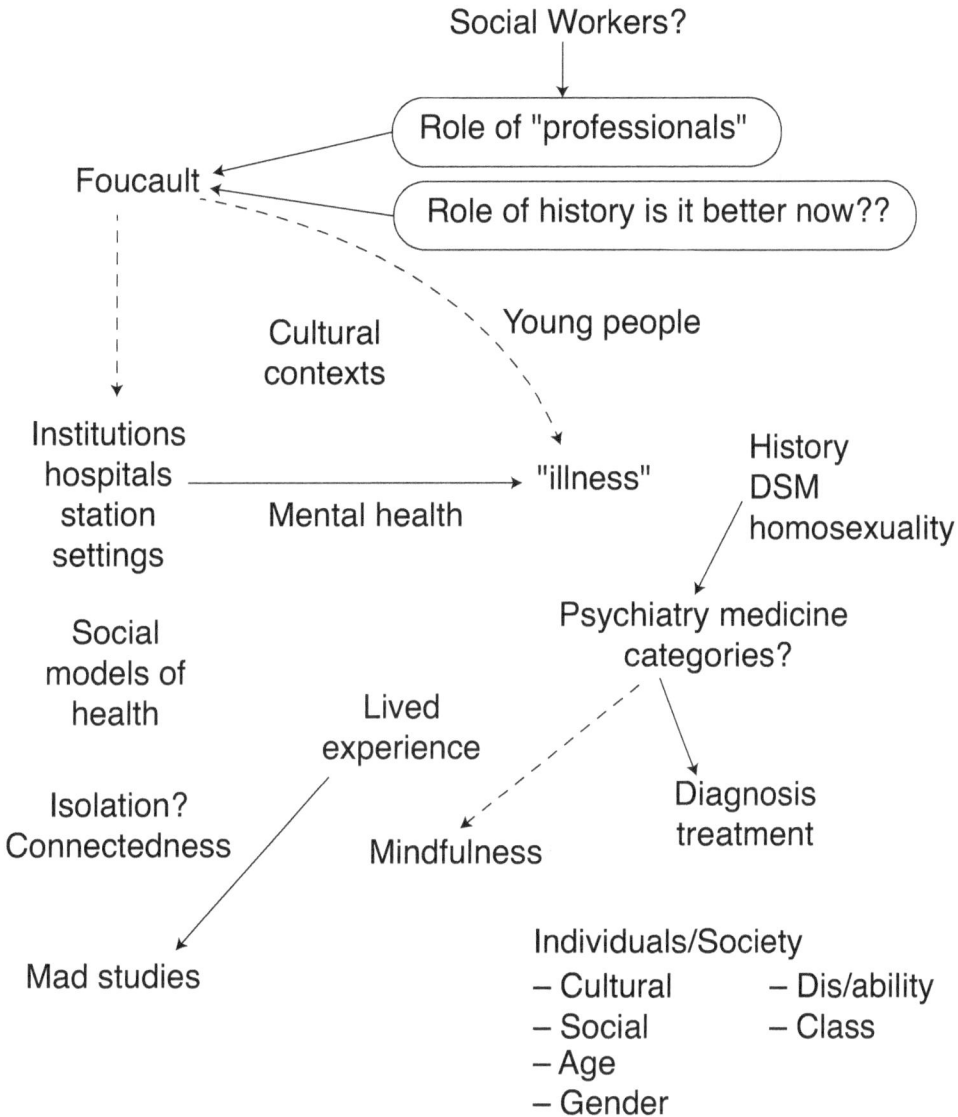

Figure 3.1 Mapping research areas and narrowing down

When looking at the map, the following questions are useful:

• What are the key debates or themes relating to research in this area?
• How has research changed over time?
• What area is of the most interest to me?
• What role does the researcher need to have in working to better understand this area of research?
• Is the researcher part of the community or group of people to whom the research is relevant?

The next step is to highlight or circle the area that will form the basis for the research project. Here, it becomes clear that a researcher cannot undertake a research project that covers *all* of the areas in Figure 3.1. This is the reality of research: narrowing down is a crucial step to take before the formulation of a research question.

Is the Question Answerable?

Vague or philosophical questions may be tempting to ask, but this is usually because we are trying to do too much with the research. Asking a question like 'What is the meaning of life?' may seem appealing and have the necessary depth for a study; however, it would be almost impossible to ask that question and find an answer. This is where it is important to think about the potential participants for a study. For example, if we are interested in the ways in which young people find meaning in their lives, this moves more towards a narrowing down of the research question and away from a vague or unfocused research question. This points to the importance of the 'who' in the research. To whom might this research be applied? What group are we wanting to hear from? Thinking about the 'where' is also going to narrow down the research focus. Where might the young people reside, for example? In a rural or remote setting or in an urban setting? What national setting might the young people be in? We can see that we are beginning to narrow down the 'who' and the 'where', which, in turn, will help us come up with an 'answerable' research question.

Understanding Limited Scope

Setting up the research to be answerable is crucial to a well-defined research question. In qualitative research, we want to find an answer to the research question that goes beyond a 'yes' or 'no' answer to the research. Staying with the example, if we are interested in the ways in which young people find meaning in their lives, we can narrow down the research question by defining and clarifying as follows:

Define	*Clarify*
What do we mean by young people?	Specify an age range
What region?	Specify a country, region, community
What is the purpose of the research?	Specify if the research is to advance understanding, counter existing narratives or address a research problem identified by the community in question
What do we mean by 'meaningful'?	Specify whether we are interested in the ways in which young people find satisfaction in their lives OR look positively towards the future OR feel content and/or happy

Once we have made decisions about the scope of the study, we can begin to see that the research question becomes more specific and therefore achievable.

Funded Research

Sometimes, research questions will be limited because the scope of the research is dictated by a funding body. For example, a piece of research may be funded by an organisation and will have limitations on what the research can achieve. Given that many research projects commence in this way, the process of designing a research question will differ slightly from the process described thus far. However, the points made earlier in the chapter around the role of power, the ways in which research can serve to oppress certain groups and the importance of ethical considerations remain. In funded research, much of the narrowing down may have already commenced. Funded research will be interested in a particular cohort of people (the 'who' question) and often will dictate to whom the research applies (the 'where' of the research is located). For example, if research is funded by a government body, there may be policy and previous research that point to a need for further exploration to service the needs of particular people. Let's imagine that we are applying for research funding which is targeted towards investigating the mental health needs of older people living at home. The process of designing a research question involves refining and clarifying and referring to the funding guidelines, as we can see in what follows.

Refine	*Clarify*
Target population	What does the funder mean by 'older people'? What does the funder mean by 'mental health'? Does 'older people' include people from all genders, cultural groups, dis/abilities? What limitations are there about where the research might take place geographically?

Taking into account the limits set by the funding body, the research question will form through understanding the limited scope of the population, that is, toward whom the research is targeted. Let's say that the funding body is interested in the mental health needs in relation to depression and anxiety of older people aged over 70 years. The funding may be directed towards research which seeks to better service people over 70 years who are socially isolated in rural communities. Just like with other processes for formulating research questions, the process will involve looking at existing research and knowledge and looking for a gap in knowledge. Perhaps it is known that people aged over 70 years are more likely to feel socially isolated than people in other age categories. It may be that there has been little research that explores the experiences for people over 70 years in rural areas in the country in which the research is to take place. Thus, the research question will be created accordingly. One example might be: What are the mental health needs of people aged over 70 years living in rural England? This research question doesn't mention gender, which would further narrow down the question. Additionally, it doesn't specify what is meant by 'mental health needs'. Further clarifying whether the research explores people with a mental health diagnosis (such as depression and anxiety) will enable the researcher to focus on a particular group of people.

Evaluation Research

Let's now think about another form of inquiry: evaluation. Evaluation can seek to better understand how services meet the needs of service users, and in social work, this can be particularly important, because organisations need to know that the services they deliver are helpful to clients.

Though seemingly straightforward, the relationship between evaluation and research is fairly contested, as noted by Wanzer, who also notes the difficulty with defining evaluation: "The lack of clear consensus of what constitutes evaluation has made it difficult to communicate what evaluation is to others outside the field" (Wanzer, 2021). Putting aside definitions for the time being, we can note the use of evaluation in social work and human service provision, and broadly speaking, we can begin with seeing evaluation as being associated with measuring the efficacy of a programme or service. We can also recognise that evaluation has a long history in social work and, notwithstanding the challenges around being 'evidence based' (Richard & Yvonne, 2018), evaluation can be approached with a critical lens (Cree et al., 2019). So what is the issue with evaluation, and why does it appear controversial?

The use of evaluation to measure efficacy has been critiqued for its Western methodologies and assumptions (Velez et al., 2022) as well as for its increased use in neoliberal service settings where social work practice is commodified and assessed to maximise cost savings (see Morley et al., 2017). These critiques need to be taken into account when designing a research question that will shape an evaluation. For example, cultural knowledge is important to consider alongside the people to whom the evaluation matters (for example, organisations, service users and practitioners). Wehipeihana argues, for example, that evaluations for Indigenous programmes should not be led by non-Indigenous evaluators (Wehipeihana, 2019). Additionally, the purpose of the evaluation needs to be clearly understood. The following questions are designed to help to shape the design of an evaluation:

- Why is the evaluation taking place?
- Who is funding the evaluation?
- What knowledge or lived experience does the evaluation team or leader have, and what is their position in relation to the service or programme being evaluated?
- How will service-user experiences be centred?
- What is the relationship between the evaluator and the service or programme?
- What does efficacy or success look like, and who gets to define this?
- Where will the results of the evaluation be communicated?
- Will there be resultant changes to a service or programme that draw from the evaluation? If so, what are the effects of this?

The ethical, social, cultural and political contexts in which research takes place have been explored in this chapter, and a research question or questions relating to evaluation must also take these contexts into account.

Conclusion

In this chapter, we have considered how social research is shaped by a range of factors including social, political, cultural and historical contexts. Deep, critical thinking about the research area has been presented as an important process in which the research question is formulated. We have explored practical strategies to help narrow down an area of focus for a research question and the ways in which research makes a small contribution to knowledge. Getting the research question 'right' will help set the foundation for research, and it is the research question that leads the researcher to design a study to generate data which will 'answer' the research question. In the following chapter, we now move on to consider research ethics in further detail.

Further Reading

Alston, M. (2020). Chapter 3: Developing research questions. In *Research for social workers: An introduction to methods*. Routledge.

Clark, T., Foster, L., Bryman, A., & Sloan, L. (2021). *Bryman's social research methods*. Oxford University Press.

Rawsthorne, M., Tseris, E., Howard, A., Terare, M., & Sharma, A. (2023). *Using social research for social justice: An introduction for social work and human services*. Taylor & Francis.

Stinchcombe, A. L. (2020). *The logic of social research*. University of Chicago Press.

References

Beresford, P. (2020). 'Mad', Mad studies and advancing inclusive resistance. *Disability & Society*, *35*(8), 1337–1342. https://doi.org/10.1080/09687599.2019.1692168

Cree, V., Jain, S., & Hillen, D. P. (2019). Evaluating effectiveness in social work: Sharing dilemmas in practice [Article]. *European Journal of Social Work*, *22*(4), 599–610. https://doi.org/10.1080/13691457.2018.1441136

Foucault, M. (2006). *Madness and civilisation: A history of insanity in the age of reason* (J. K. Jonathan Murphy, Trans.). Routledge.

Lenza, M. (2004). Controversies surrounding Laud Humphreys' tearoom trade: An unsettling example of politics and power in methodological critiques. *International Journal of Sociology and Social Policy*, *24*(3/4/5), 20–31. https://doi.org/10.1108/01443330410790858

Morley, C., MacFarlane, S., & Ablett, P. (2017). The neoliberal colonisation of social work education: A critical analysis and practices for resistance. *Advances in Social Work and Welfare Education*, *19*(2). https://ezproxy.deakin.edu.au/login?url=https://search.ebscohost.com/login.aspx?direct=true&db=edsaed&AN=rmitplus219527&site=eds-live&scope=site

Richard, M. G., Jr., & Yvonne, A. U. (2018). *Social work research and evaluation: Foundations of evidence-based practice* (Vol. Eleventh edition) [Book]. Oxford University Press. https://ezproxy.deakin.edu.au/login?url=https://search.ebscohost.com/login.aspx?direct=true&db=nlebk&AN=1701929&site=eds-live&scope=site

Serrano Amaya, J. F., & Ríos González, O. (2019). Introduction to the special issue: Challenges of LGBT research in the 21st century. *International Sociology*, *34*(4), 371–381. https://doi.org/10.1177/0268580919856490

Velez, C., Nuechterlein, B., Connors, S., RedShirt Tyon, G., Roane, T. M., & Mays, D. C. (2022). Application of the Indigenous evaluation framework to a University certificate program for building cultural awareness in science, technology, engineering, and mathematics. *Evaluation and Program Planning*, *92*, 102066. https://doi.org/10.1016/j.evalprogplan.2022.102066

Wanzer, D. L. (2021). What is evaluation?: Perspectives of how evaluation differs (or Not) from research. *American Journal of Evaluation*, *42*(1), 28–46. https://doi.org/10.1177/1098214020920710

Wehipeihana, N. (2019). Increasing cultural competence in support of indigenous-led evaluation: A necessary step toward indigenous-led evaluation [Article]. *Canadian Journal of Program Evaluation*, *34*(2), 368–384. https://doi.org/10.3138/cjpe.68444

4   Research Ethics

Chapter Summary

- Social justice provides an ethical lens for the researcher.
- Using a social justice lens allows the researcher to reflect on fairness and inequalities in society and the subsequent positioning of the research area.
- History provides examples of unethical research; however, understanding research ethics ought to be viewed as an ongoing project.
- Ethical codes of conduct provide guidance about measures to mitigate harm but should not be the only point at which ethics are considered.
- Research ethics are connected to the aims of critical qualitative research.

Introduction

In Chapter 3, we began to introduce ethics alongside considerations of the research question by arguing that the asking of a research question is connected to assumptions, values and social attitudes. We also argued that social, political, cultural and historical contexts ought to be considered when asking a research question because of our ethical responsibilities to the people with whom we work. In this chapter, we expand upon the ways in which ethical approaches are important at the beginning of a research project, where we might be considering the research question. Throughout this book we show that ethics are important to the design of social research, the methods used to generate data to answer the research question as well as the ways in which the research findings are disseminated. To think about research ethics is not only to understand the responsibilities of the researcher but also to expand ethics to be a system which influences relationships between knowledge holders and researchers (George et al., 2020). Utilising social work ethics in research enables critical reflexivity for the researcher as well as enabling research processes and decisions to be answerable to ethical justifications. This requires knowledge about ethics and includes examining the lessons we have learned about unethical research. The chapter commences by positioning the power that social research has in emancipatory aims by taking a social justice lens. We then move on to explore what we can learn from unethical research. We conclude by exploring the ways in which research positions knowledge holders and explore the emergence of lived experience and peer-based research.

Social Justice

Social justice is a concept rooted in philosophical questions about the ways in which society distributes its resources, and its burdens, to individuals. A socially just society is

DOI: 10.4324/9781003316732-4

one in which there is fairness in the equitable distribution of resources, and social justice is a foundational and well-established perspective that underpins social work in contemporary times (Austin, 2013; Baines, 2011; Taylor et al., 2017). Understanding patterns of inequality, that is, the shared characteristics of people to whom resources are more or less available, is an important aspect to social justice. Put simply, it is not just or fair that certain groups of people with a shared characteristic are disadvantaged. Shared characteristics can include gender, sexual identity, culture, race, age, dis/ability and so on, and so it follows that because someone is a *man* that he ought to earn more than a woman or someone who is gender non-binary for the same work. Here, the shared characteristic of gender is used to demonstrate the principles of justice and fairness. Throughout this book, we argue that social research has the potential to bring about positive social change through a commitment to social justice and the careful orientation of situating research problems in their social, historical, cultural and political contexts. Denzin articulates the potential for transformative and emancipatory research and argues that, historically speaking, the time for this kind of research is now:

> What is the role of critical qualitative research in a historical present when the need for social justice has never been greater? This is a historical present that cries out for emancipatory visions, for visions that inspire transformative inquiries, for inquiries that can provide the moral authority to move people to struggle and resist oppression. We need to work through a politics of critical inquiry that embraces all components of social justice inquiry.
>
> (Denzin, 2018, p. 101)

Maintaining a social justice lens is an important in research because it allows us to draw out power imbalances and consider the question: Who benefits and who suffers? Research should not induce suffering but should bring about positive change. Just as with social work, research is not a value-free activity. We can see throughout history that a great deal of harm has been done in the name of research, which we will now briefly explore in order to understand our ethical responsibilities as critical social researchers.

History's Lessons: Research-Induced Harm

As we said, it is important to understand how we came to appreciate some of the core ethical principles involved in designing research today. The harm that research can inflict upon human subjects is documented through what we now consider to be unethical examples of research, and alongside these historical events, we can see the ways in which power was exercised by the people who carried out what can only be thought about as harmful in the name of advancing scientific knowledge. We can also see the ways in which the researcher as 'expert' reinforces a power inequality between the expert and the 'research subject'.

The following material is confronting and likely distressing. We include it here so that the reader can consider the question: Who benefits and who suffers from research? These are difficult examples to read about, but they illustrate the most extreme harm and torture that can be inflicted and attempted to be justified in the name of research.

During the Second World War in Nazi Germany, scientists conducted painful, inhumane and lethal experiments on prisoners. For example, these included:

> High-altitude experiments . . . Conducted for the German air force to investigate the effect of high-altitude flying; experiments were conducted at the Dachau camp

using a low-pressure chamber. . . . Freezing experiments . . . Conducted primarily for the German air force to investigate treatments for persons who had been severely chilled, using prisoners at the Dachau camp . . . Malaria experiments . . . Conducted to test immunization for and treatment of malaria; experiments were conducted on more than 1000 prisoners at Dachau.

(Freckelton, 2009, p. 560)

In addition, research experiments were inflicted on prisoners through exposure to mustard gas as well as the deliberate infliction of wounds and burns to test the efficacy of treatments. Bone, muscle and nerve surgery and transplants were also performed on incarcerated people in camps (Freckelton, 2009). We know that the people sent to concentration camps or killed in Nazi Germany were what we might think about in contemporary society as minority groups: Jewish people, queer/LGBT people, disabled people (Goeschel & Wachsmann, 2010; Knittel, 2014; Whisnant, 2016).

The Holocaust was influential on the development of bioethics because of the Nuremberg Trials, which saw some of the medical personnel who tortured and murdered people in the name of research charged for their crimes against humanity, and this led to the development of the Nuremberg Code (Freckelton, 2009). It seems obvious in contemporary society that the experiments conducted on people in Nazi Germany were unethical because they amounted to torture, people could not consent to participate and harm was inflicted upon people. Let us now consider another example of unethical research.

The Tuskegee syphilis experiment was medical research involving around 400 participants who were not told about the purpose of the study. The study ran from 1932 to 1972, and participants were denied treatment for syphilis even though antibiotics were discovered to be effective in the treatment of syphilis during the course of the study. The people recruited for the experiment were working-class African American men whose syphilis was left deliberately untreated, and instead, their symptoms were clinically observed over time (Schütz & Braswell, 2023). Syphilis, left untreated, is a painful degenerative disease that leads to death.

It is easy to say that such horrific examples of research are a product of their times and that given what we now know about research ethics, such atrocities would never again occur because we have an understanding that people who participate in research are volunteers, and researchers should not inflict harm. Research ethics committees scrutinise proposed research in a range of settings including universities, medical settings and practice settings and organisations. Yet there is likely to be research occurring today that we may consider unethical either now or in the future. For example, research on people in prisons continues to occur, though participants may be paid (see Hornblum, 1998). Ethics committees and codes of conduct should not be viewed as detracting from the personal responsibilities of the researcher (Bauman, 1993). We agree with the following quotation that positions the researcher as requiring to know the difference between research for positive outcomes and research that harms:

A culture of rights incorporates making moral judgments from time to time. This involves naming some conduct as wrong, discriminatory, rights-incompatible and, sometimes, where it is sufficiently offensive, as 'evil'. It means that we need to refrain from the comfort of moral relativism in relation to such ascriptions and from retreating into the safe shores of contextualism to understand such behaviour. In respect of the execution of innocent persons and imposing harmful testing procedures upon them without their consent, while many at the time may have been able to rationalise the conduct, it means acknowledging this was ethically repugnant behaviour that was incompatible with being a medical practitioner and deserves unreserved castigation. If this means employing the moralistic and emotive descriptor 'evil', so be it.

(Freckelton, 2009, p. 566)

Critical Research for Social Change

There is much to be said about risk in the contemporary world (Beck, 1992; Beck, 1999), as social workers working in statutory settings know only too well (Stanford, 2010). In research, risks to participant well-being can emerge as a consequence of the researcher investigating sensitive or personal matters and asking participants, for example, to recount distressing experiences. However, the researcher doesn't need to avoid risk completely, as Israel notes: "Usually, researchers should try to avoid imposing even the *risk* of harm on others. Of course, most research involves some risk, generally at a level greater in magnitude than the minimal risk we tend to encounter in our everyday lives" (Israel, 2015, p. 125). Risks to participant well-being are usually mitigated by researcher actions such as ensuring that participants understand what they are consenting to in participating in the research as well as offering support services in the event that a participant is distressed through the research.

In critical research, it could be argued that risks *should* be taken but that these risks do not negatively impact the research population or participants. For example, a researcher taking a stance against the reproduction of oppression or discrimination or using their platform to amplify voices of people who have been traditionally silenced might be considered risky. Risk is therefore an example of the need to conceptualise research that recognises the impacts of somewhat mechanistic processes related to ethics (Bauman, 1993) but considers the research, including researchers, in their critical contexts. This also includes understanding the history of research with a particular population. Western research is arguably only just grappling with the harms caused by undertaking research 'on' Indigenous communities and positioning the researcher as the holder of knowledge (George et al., 2020, p. 5; Ife & Tascon, 2016). As we further discuss in Chapter 9, the researcher ought to reject binary notions of power such as seeing people as *powerful* or *powerless* and instead reflect upon the ways that researchers (as so-called experts) and the people with whom we research, access power (Foucault, 2006). Western ethics processes "continue to uphold a relationality between the role of researcher as protector of ethics and the vulnerable Indigenous person as the subject of protection" (Sherwood & Anthony in (George et al., 2020, p. 20). As Bennett argues, colonisation has produced a research system that undervalues and ignores Indigenous knowledges, practices and worldviews (Bennett, 2020).

Let's now consider this a little further in thinking about the ways in which knowledge is positioned in research and explore the ethical implications of this and how researchers can approach critical research with this understanding.

Knowledge Holders and an Ethic of Collaboration

Whereas contemporary research ethics situate the researcher as the 'expert' (Bennett, 2020), we have seen the emergence of critical research which seeks to position knowledge expertise away from the researcher. This recognises that

[T]here is the assumption that the colonial subject has nothing directly of interest to impart; it is the 'expert' white knowledge-maker who knows the 'real' knowledge that is to be extracted from the empty vessel, and thus knowledge always has to be interpreted by that white expert.

(Bennett, 2020, p. 53)

In social work and social science research, we see the beginnings (historically speaking) of a recognition of the concept of expertise through lived experience. This positions knowledge, power relations and ethics through the context of co-production in the research process (Storm, 2023). Similarly, the term 'peer-based' research refers to researchers being situated within the communities in which research takes place. The maxim 'nothing about us without us', for example, is a research methodology in sex work research, which has traditionally been undertaken by non–sex workers (Diamond et al., 2022; Lobo et al., 2021). This connects to the way that we frame our ethical commitment to social justice in critical research. As discussed in Chapter 3, the asking of a research question is a powerful act because it frames the ways in which the researcher values the knowledge of the people with whom they are researching.

Critical research is research in which the researcher considers their own position and location within the research area and sees the research as being a co-production (Franklin & Franklin, 2021). Such an approach recognises the historical (and present) harms that research can inflict but also, importantly, positions people with lived experience as those with expertise.

Conclusion

In this chapter, we have begun to orient the beginning researcher to research ethics. By examining clear examples of unethical research in an historical context, we have explored participation in research, consent to participate and the potential for research to do harm. We have also considered research ethics processes and the responsibilities of the researcher who wants to undertake research that has a positive social impact. This chapter is foundational in terms of thinking about how social justice provides an ethical orientation to research, and in the following chapters, we further explore how to achieve this.

Further Reading

Hölscher, D., Hugman, R., & McAuliffe, D. (2023). *Social work theory and ethics ideas in practice*. Springer Nature Singapore.
Ife, J., & Tascon, S. M. (2016). Human rights and critical social work: Competing epistemologies for practice. *Social Alternatives*, 35(4), 27–31.
Taylor, S., Vreugdenhil, A., & Schneiders, M. (2017). Social justice as concept and practice in Australian social work: An analysis of Norma Parker addresses, 1969–2008. *Australian Social Work*, 70(Suppl 1), 46–68.

References

Austin, M. J. (2013). *Social justice and social work: Rediscovering a core value of the profession*. SAGE Publications.
Baines, D. (2011). *Doing anti-oppressive practice: Social justice social work* (2nd ed.). Fernwood Pub.
Bauman, Z. (1993). *Postmodern ethics*. Blackwell.
Beck, U. (1992). *Risk society: Towards a new modernity*. Sage.

Beck, U. (1999). *World risk society*. Polity Press.

Bennett, B. (2020). Acknowledgements in Aboriginal social work research: How to counteract neo-liberal academic complacency. In S. M. Tascon & J. Ife (Eds.), *Disrupting whiteness in social work*. Routledge/Taylor and Francis Group.

Denzin, N. K. (2018). *The qualitative manifesto: A call to arms*. Routledge.

Diamond, R., Dunk-West, P., & Wendt, S. (2022). Using sex worker feminism in practice to promote a peer-based methodology: Exploring personal and professional identities in a research alliance centring sex worker lived experience. In C. Cocker & T. Hafford-Letchfield (Eds.), *Rethinking feminist theories for social work practice*. Palgrave Macmillan.

Foucault, M. (2006). *Madness and civilisation: A history of insanity in the age of reason* (J. K. Jonathan Murphy, Trans.). Routledge.

Franklin, A., & Franklin, A. (2021). *Co-creativity and engaged scholarship: Transformative methods in social sustainability research*. Springer Nature.

Freckelton, I. (2009). Bioethics, biopolitics and medical regulation: Learning from the Nazi doctor experience. *Journal of law and Medicine*, 16(4), 555–567.

George, L., Tauri, J., & MacDonald, T. A. o. T. L. (2020). *Indigenous research ethics: Claiming research sovereignty beyond deficit and the colonial legacy*. Emerald Publishing.

Goeschel, C., & Wachsmann, N. (2010). Before Auschwitz: The formation of the Nazi concentration camps, 1933–1939. *Journal of Contemporary History*, 45(3), 515–534. https://doi.org/10.1177/0022009410366554

Hornblum, A. M. (1998). *Acres of skin human experiments at Holmesburg Prison: A story of abuse and exploitation in the name of medical science*. Routledge.

Ife, J., & Tascon, S. M. (2016). Human rights and critical social work: Competing epistemologies for practice. *Social Alternatives*, 35(4), 27–31.

Israel, M. A. (2015). *Research ethics and integrity for social scientists: Beyond regulatory compliance/Mark Israel* (2nd ed.). SAGE.

Knittel, S. C. (2014). *The historical uncanny: Disability, ethnicity, and the politics of holocaust memory* (1st ed.). Fordham University Press. https://doi.org/10.1515/9780823262809

Lobo, R., McCausland, K., Bates, J., Hallett, J., Donovan, B., & Selvey, L. A. (2021). Sex workers as peer researchers – a qualitative investigation of the benefits and challenges. *Culture, Health & Sexuality*, 23(10), 1435–1450. https://doi.org/10.1080/13691058.2020.1787520

Schütz, M., & Braswell, H. (2023). Ethicizing history. Bioethical representations of Nazi medicine. *Bioethics*, 37(6), 581–590. https://doi.org/10.1111/bioe.13168

Stanford, S. (2010). 'Speaking back' to fear: Responding to the moral dilemmas of risk in social work practice. *The British Journal of Social Work*, 40(4), 1065–1080. https://doi.org/10.1093/bjsw/bcp156

Storm, P. (2023). Lived experiences as a starting point for social work research – possibilities and challenges. *The British Journal of Social Work*, 53(3), 1801–1808. https://doi.org/10.1093/bjsw/bcad035

Taylor, S., Vreugdenhil, A., & Schneiders, M. (2017). Social justice as concept and practice in Australian social work: An analysis of Norma Parker addresses, 1969–2008. *Australian Social Work*, 70(Suppl 1), 46–68. https://doi.org/10.1080/0312407X.2014.973554

Whisnant, C. J. (2016). *Queer identities and politics in Germany: A history, 1880–1945*. Harrington Park Press.

5　The Literature Review

Chapter Summary

- In the context of social research, 'literature' refers to written pieces, often scholarly, such as peer-reviewed journals, or those of artistic or intellectual significance.
- A literature review is crucial in research to inform both readers and researchers about established knowledge, strengths, weaknesses and relationships between sources, providing a solid foundation for our research.
- Our job in reviewing the literature is to critically evaluate the relevance and significance of such written content, applying our social justice lens to interrogate potential research bias and to reflect on questions of power, positionality and authenticity.
- Writing a literature review is a skill that involves thorough reading, note-taking, and organisation of existing literature and the construction of a logically flowing narrative that contributes to scholarly conversation.

Introduction

A literature review is an important step in the research process because it helps both the reader and the researcher preparing the review be better informed about what knowledge and ideas have been established on a topic and what their strengths and weaknesses might be. The goal of a literature review should be to critically analyse the evidence, or knowledge base, that already exists in the area you are researching (Dekkers et al., 2022). It looks for relationships between different literature sources and provides a solid foundation for your own research. It identifies any gaps in the literature that your research can fill and highlights the relevance of your research in the context of existing knowledge. It also shows to others, for example, funding bodies, industry stakeholders, community representatives, that you are well informed and knowledgeable with regards to contemporary social issues. Given we live in an information-saturated world, prioritising sources for your literature review is particularly important (Ruan, 2016). As such, this chapter covers how to access, rank and evaluate sources, as well as considering deeper questions as to who is controlling the narrative when it comes to published information and 'evidence'. This chapter presents tools and strategies for how to synthesise information, group information and knowledge claims and construct an argument. Using examples from practitioners and research students, this chapter demonstrates the relevance of literature reviews in diverse practice contexts as well as encouraging the reader to develop their own argument and confident writing voice.

DOI: 10.4324/9781003316732-5

Getting Started

Starting a literature review can be quite overwhelming, particularly when you feel like you don't know where to start. That's okay! Part of the purpose of a literature review is to stimulate thought on the research topic and start to narrow down your focus based on what is known or not known. Because it can be easy to get distracted and go down a rabbit warren of interesting information, this chapter encourages us to approach the literature-review process in a systematic, step-by-step way from the initial data search through to evaluation and writing up your review. However, we also recognise that few things in life, and this includes research, are ever linear. When approaching the literature review and broadening your knowledge on a certain topic, it is okay to go back and refine your original research questions or ideas. This reflects an iterative approach that is responsive and well informed. The goal of the literature review is to feel confident about summarising the key debates, concepts and any gaps, in large part so as to justify the need for further research.

Researcher Reflection

My name is Jaimie, and I am currently a PhD candidate and research assistant at Charles Darwin University. Reflecting on my first experiences of social work research, my memory is flooded with an overwhelm of unfamiliar, complicated and somewhat intimidating research terminology. I was completing a master of social work, and my first field placement was during the peak of COVID-19 lockdowns. I was placed in an online field placement so that my degree was not interrupted by the global closures, but I was disappointed that I would not get to experience 'real social work' during this time. My supervisor suggested I attempt a research proposal as part of my placement, with the first step to complete a literature review on my chosen topic. I had certainly heard of a literature review, and the concept seemed simple at first. That was until I started reading the literature on how to write a research proposal. Epistemology, ontology, methodology . . . What had I got myself in to? These words seemed so foreign, and much of the literature I read to understand them only led to further confusion. Regardless, I began my first attempt at a literature review. I had my research question, and I began to search the various databases, eager to present my findings to my supervisor. I had certainly read widely on my topic. I presented the main themes in the literature and understood the various methodologies used, and my literature review was reasonably well written. There was just one issue: my supervisor asked me, "So what?"

Throughout my studies, assignments generally consisted of answering a question or speaking to a topic. What I had failed to understand was that the purpose of this literature review was to support a research proposal and justify the need for further research by critically evaluating the current literature and identifying the gaps in the current knowledge. While this may seem like a simple concept, it was the confusion around the purpose of the literature review that had made it a difficult process for me (and, I have since learned, for many other students). With the understanding of the purpose and importance of a literature review, I have since undertaken many

> *more, and it has become one of my favourite parts of the research process. Not only do you gain such a wide understanding in your area of interest, but you also become experienced at identifying what is missing and become naturally curious about what can be done to strengthen our understanding and make a contribution to research within your field.*

What Do We Mean by 'Literature'?

When we refer to the term 'literature', we quite literally mean written pieces of work. Literature studies, for example, involves the study of written prose considered of artistic, cultural and/or intellectual significance. In the context of conducting a literature review within social research, we are evaluating written content considered of significance or relevance to our topic. This tends to come in a variety of scholarly sources and reputable reports; although not all sources are considered reliable or credible, being able to apply your analytical skills and discern between sources is a key expectation when conducting a literature review, and we examine this process later in this chapter. You may find it helpful to draw from the following types of sources when undertaking a literature review:

Peer-Reviewed Articles in Scholarly Journals

Peer-reviewed articles are generally considered the most credible and reliable sources of information when conducting a literature review. This is because they are generally written and prepared by academics who then submit their publication for review by other academics (hence the term 'peer reviewed') to ensure a high standard of quality. The review process is normally anonymous, that is, neither the reviewer nor the person submitting the article knows the name of one another. The reviewers may recommend minor or major changes, including more details about the methodological process or ethical considerations, or they may recommend that the paper be rejected and not published. Scholarly journals are also ranked, with those considered more reputable being given a higher ranking than others. For this reason, peer-reviewed articles are generally the 'go-to' when beginning a literature review. However, it is important to keep in mind that because of the lengthy process of review prior to publication, there can be delays in the timeline between when a piece of research has been completed and when the results are disseminated (Walter, 2019).

Textbooks and Edited Books

Designed to facilitate understanding for students, textbooks offer condensed and simplified renditions of research. While they serve as useful introductory resources, they may not capture the full depth and nuance of original reports. They can be useful for providing definitions of key terms or providing conceptual clarity. They often also provide references to the original sources of information with which readers can then locate and engage. Wherever possible, when conducting a literature review, it is important to use the original source.

Edited books are also another useful source of information. These books are generally composed of multiple chapters on a particular topic/area, with each chapter written by a different author. These books are often reviewed and evaluated by the editor prior to going to publication. Similar to the delays that can occur in the peer-review process within journal article publication, the same can also occur with edited books, which impacts how recent some of the findings might be? They are informative and useful resources, and although it has become more and more common for edited texts to be available online, some books may only be available in hard copy. This also depends on the type of library access you have and whether your library has purchased an electronic or hard copy.

Monographs

A monograph is a scholarly work that provides an in-depth and comprehensive examination of a specific subject or topic. Unlike edited books that may feature chapters from various authors, a monograph is typically the product of a single author's sustained research and analysis. It is characterised by its detailed exploration, often presenting original insights, interpretations or arguments within a specific field of study. These are often very large bodies of work. However, they can be useful with regards to preparing a literature review and to gaining further understanding of how a research methodology is applied.

Grey Literature

'Grey literature' is a name given to research or information materials that are not formally published through traditional academic channels, such as peer-reviewed journals or commercial publishers. This category includes reports, working papers, conference proceedings and other types of documents produced by organisations, government agencies, think tanks or research institutions. Grey literature may not undergo the same rigorous peer-review processes as traditional scholarly publications, so it is important to take into consideration the authorship. For example, organisations such as the United Nations or International Monetary Fund are generally considered reputable organisations, whereas some state-run organisations in countries with questionable reporting practices may not carry as much weight. Generally speaking, organisational reports from institutions with a high level of transparency (including detail as to how the data was collected) can be valuable for providing insights, data or perspectives that may not be readily available through conventional academic sources. Be wary of content that doesn't provide clear information as to who the authors are or from tabloid press outlets whose goal is to sell newspapers/magazines for profit (rather than to undergo rigorous and methodical fact-checking). Media pieces can be useful with regards to assessing dominant discourse and public attitudes towards a certain social phenomenon or issue, but they should not be used as a substitute for a rigorous and systematic review of other available literature sources.

Accessing and Locating Sources

Although you may refine your question slightly as your knowledge of a topic expands, it can be helpful to set clear parameters with regards to your literature review to avoid getting distracted by literature sources that, although interesting, are not specifically of benefit to your own research question. Being able to articulate a research question that informs your literature review will assist in providing clarity, focus and direction to the inquiry while ensuring that the review aligns with the broader goals of the research study (Lockwood et al., 2020; Peters et al., 2020). It may also assist in developing your key search terms. Being able to accurately search databases for relevant data is a key research skill, and most libraries will offer training or support to assist you in developing your search strategy. A simple example of how you might develop a search strategy is outlined in the following table. However, a plethora of books and online resources also provide further instruction on how to refine your search strategy (see Further Reading).

Developing a Search Strategy Template

Steps	*Search Strategy*		
1 Write down your topic or research question.			
2 Select Keywords from your topic.	Keyword One: Keyword Two:		
	Keyword Three:		
3 Based on the keywords you identified, select synonyms or similar words.	Keyword One	Synonym	Synonym
	Keyword Two	Synonym	Synonym
	Keyword Three	Synonym	Synonym
4 Formulate a search strategy using Boolean operators (AND, OR) to connect your keywords.	AND	OR OR	OR OR

Example completed search strategy template

Steps	*Search Strategy*		
1 Write down your topic or research question.	*Young people and recreational drug use* *What are young people's views about the use of recreational party drugs?*		
2 Select Keywords from your topic.	Keyword One: Young people		
	Keyword Two: Drugs Keyword Three: Recreation		
3 Based on the keywords you identified, select synonyms or similar words.	Keyword One: *Young people*	Synonym: *Adolescent*	Synonym: *Teenager*
	Keyword Two: *Illicit substances*	Synonym: *Illegal drugs*	Synonym *Illicit drugs*
	Keyword Three: *Recreational*	Synonym *Party*	Synonym: *Festival*
4 Formulate a search strategy using Boolean operators (AND, OR) to connect your keywords.	*"Young people"* OR *Adolescent** OR *Teen** *AND*		
	"Illicit substance*" OR *"Illegal drug*"* OR *"Illicit drug*"* *AND*		
	Recreation* OR *Party* OR *Festival**		

Potential Search Database

Potential Databases

Databases: Medicine/Nursing	Databases: Social Sciences	Grey Literature
ProQuest	Sociological Abstracts	Dissertations Abstracts
Informit	Sociology Source Ultimate	.gov
Google Scholar	Global Health	.org
JSTOR	WHO Regional indices	
Cochrane	PAIS index	
PsycINFO	Other:	
Web of Science	Other:	
Scopus		
MEDLINE (e.g. PubMed)		
ERIC		
Other:		
Other:		

Practitioner Reflection

My name is Bec. I am a sexual assault support worker and have been with my current community-based organisation for the past three years. Literature reviews are something I first learned about in my third year of university during my social work degree. At the time, I thought that literature reviews were just another complicated academic process that would not be helpful for everyday practice. My assumptions were based on the fact that I have struggled to understand academic language and processes in general. Since engaging in a research unit through my studies, I have had an opportunity to undertake numerous literature reviews and have found them to be supportive in helping to identify gaps in research and advocate for the women I support through my practice. Having the ability to use literature reviews as a tool for advocacy has supported my ability to provide a summary of key conclusions relating to arguments on topics, including when appearing in court or advocating at a policy or systemic level. I have also supported students in my organisation to conduct literature reviews as a means of contributing to and keeping up to date with relevant research and best practice in the field of sexual violence. Currently, my organisation is undergoing a comprehensive service evaluation in order to improve service delivery with persons from gender-diverse and/or non–English-speaking backgrounds. In reflection, this process could have been better supported and more efficient had we undertaken a literature review as a foundational starting point rather than steaming ahead with surveys without first doing the groundwork. A literature review would have revealed a lot of what is considered 'best practice' and also provided guidance about how best to engage in research with communities to ensure the evaluation process reflects their experiences and isn't just another case of vulnerable communities being researched on rather than with. If anyone has not used literature reviews in their practice or workplace, I would say that this is a worthy investment of time and energy. Don't be put off by the idea that it's something only fancy academics can do. Feeling confident to engage in reviewing literature has helped me to feel better informed and able to justify my actions and ethical decision-making in practice.

Critically Evaluating Sources

Once you have completed your search and have compiled a list of articles, books and resources, you inevitably have to read! While it can be tempting to skip over documents and just read the abstract or conclusion (particularly with competing priorities and looming deadlines), it is only through actually reading and engaging with the content that you can hope to develop your understanding of a topic and issues (Walter, 2019). This doesn't mean you have to read everything that has ever been written, but generally speaking, you should keep reading until you reach what is known as 'saturation', that is, the information you are reading is no longer presenting new ideas or information or shedding any new light on your topic (Morse, 2015). Most importantly, when it comes to engaging in a literature review, the purpose is not to summarise or regurgitate content but rather to demonstrate knowledge on the subject matter and to be able to articulate key areas of tension, ambiguity or debate. This requires you to be able to critically evaluate the content you are reading and to consciously reflect on the positionality and potential agenda of the evidence you are being presented. Accessing what is considered 'scholarly works' and grey literature is a great place to start, but as with all social narratives and research agendas, these were not produced in an ideological vacuum. As critical consumers of research, we need to be conscious of whose voices are being privileged in the construction of an evidence base.

What Do We Mean by 'Evidence'?

When gathering data for your literature review, you are asked to engage with the existing 'evidence base'; that is, the existing studies and research that are available on your topic. Often, the term 'empirical evidence' or 'evidence base' is used to show that there has been established research on a particular way of practising or research; for example, the use of attachment theory in child safety assessments or the application of neuro-science in understandings about trauma (Rawsthorne et al., 2023). Interestingly, just because there is a lot of information on a topic or from which a large evidence base is used to draw information doesn't mean that this should automatically be accepted as good practice or 'true'. In the examples of attachment theories and trauma theories in child protection contexts, for example, such theories have been developed by white men and applied largely in Western contexts (Choate & Tortorelli, 2022). The idea that these theories can then be applied universally and are generalisable to the larger population fails to acknowledge cultural nuance, alternative forms of parenting and raising children and divergent religious beliefs around grief and loss, and it is symptomatic of positivist and empirical research positions that assume that what is true in one context can be similarly applied in others (Crotty, 1998). Evidence-based narratives in social work practice wield considerable influence and frequently evolve into dominant discourses capable of self-replication and acceptance as truths. An uncritical acceptance of these dominant discourses reinforces a positivist paradigm and suggests it is desirable, ethical and possible for researchers and practitioners to be objective, neutral and unbiased in their engagement with others (Morley et al., 2019). Yet as we uncovered in Chapter 2, such a position fails to acknowledge the broader social context in which ideas are constructed, and the ableist, sexist, racist, ageist, colonialist and homophobic influences which impact both our work within and research about the world in which we live. If we uncritically accept information as truth without critically examining the context in which it was written, we may become complicit in perpetuating further harm, however unintentional this might be.

Scientific evidence is intricately linked to both social and cultural contexts, in addition to specific methodologies and data (Morley et al., 2019). Despite claims of generalisability and objectivity in many research paradigms, there is little research that can be said to be categorically 'true', especially from the position of social work, which values the socio-political and historical context (Dunk-West, 2018). Rawsthorne and Colleagues (2023) suggest that rather than rejecting the generalisability and trustworthiness of research publications outright, it can be useful to adopt a social justice and decolonising lens to research interpretation. Instead of uncritically accepting research findings developed through the eyes of the objective and expert researcher, a critical and social justice–informed way to assess research trustworthiness, reliability and credibility involves deliberately unpacking what we are reading and reflecting key questions.

1) *What and where are the knowledge contributions from research participants and from those impacted by the research results?*
2) *Has the research been done with or on participants?*
3) *Who owns the knowledge generated from the research?*
4) *How have participants and people impacted by the research been involved in decisions about research translation and communication?*
5) *Who wanted this research to be done and who is most likely to use it?*

(Rawsthorne et al., 2023, p. 39)

Assessing the Quality of Sources

When evaluating sources for your literature review, it's important to critically assess various aspects. First, consider the expertise of the author. Take a close look at their qualifications, institutional affiliations and previous publications. Assess whether they have conducted extensive research or have practical experience related to the topic. Next, examine the research methodology employed in the study. Evaluate whether the methodology was appropriate for addressing the research question. For qualitative research, this might involve methods like interviews, observations or content analysis. Consider factors such as data collection techniques, data ownership and data analysis methods. Look for details on how the data was gathered, recorded and interpreted. Consider whether the methods used were suitable for capturing the nuances and complexities of the research topic.

Remember, in a literature review, you're not expected to only include sources with large population samples. Qualitative research can provide valuable insights and in-depth understanding of social phenomena. Focus on the quality, ethical considerations, recognition of positionality, privileging of participant voices and relevance of the research, rather than solely on sample size. Examine the study's findings and interpretations. Consider whether the conclusions are supported by the data and whether alternative explanations or perspectives have been adequately considered. Look for any limitations or biases acknowledged by the authors. Finally, determine how relevant the source is to your own research question. Consider whether the study addresses a similar or related topic and whether the findings or insights can contribute to your own research. You may find it useful to answer this checklist in preparation for writing your own literature review.

Literature Quality Checklist

Publication Source	Is the information from a 'credible' source? Are the author and publication details easily accessible? Remember, scholarly sources often include peer-reviewed journal articles, academic books and conference proceedings authored by 'experts' in the field. High-quality and scholarly works are characterised by well-researched content, clear methodology, citations from reputable sources and a formal writing style.	Yes	☐	No	☐
Author's Expertise	Assess the author's qualifications, expertise and reputation in the field. Look for their academic credentials, institutional affiliations and previous publications. Consider whether they have conducted extensive research or have practical experience related to the topic.	Yes	☐	No	☐
Methodology	Evaluate the appropriateness and ideological alignment of the methodology for addressing the research question. Does the methodology support a social justice prerogative? Does the research position the researcher as the 'expert' or prioritise the views of participants?	Yes	☐	No	☐
Method	For qualitative research, the methods might feature interviews, observations, focus groups or content analysis. Consider factors such as sample size, data collection techniques and data analysis methods. Consider whether the methods used were appropriate for capturing the nuances and complexities of the research topic. Look for details on how the data was collected, recorded and analysed. Do the methods align with the goals and objectives of the research? Do they fit with the methodological and ideological arguments?	Yes	☐	No	☐
Findings and Data Analysis	Do the researchers identify a theoretical or conceptual framework for analysis? (This may be overt, or you may need to deduce this from the types of methodology and methods employed.) Are the claims made by the researchers supported by what the participants say or data shows? Look for any limitations or biases acknowledged by the authors.	Yes	☐	No	☐
Relevance	Determine the relevance of the source to your research question. Consider whether the study addresses a similar or related topic and whether the findings or insights can contribute to your own research. Assess how the source fits into the broader context of the literature on your topic.	Yes	☐	No	☐

Writing Your Review

Writing a literature review is a skill, because it takes time to review and evaluate existing literature (Dunk-West, 2018). To do a literature review well, you need to read! Read, read and then read some more! As you read, take good notes; highlight key findings, methodologies and any gaps or debates in the existing research. It's like creating a road map of what's out there. Then, organise those notes into themes or categories. This is where your literature review starts taking shape. Discuss how each piece of literature contributes to the broader conversation. Address the methodologies used, findings and any differences in perspectives. And don't forget to critically evaluate each source: consider the author's bias, the study's limitations and its relevance to your question. You may like to refer to the literature quality checklist.

As you write, make sure your literature review flows logically. Start with the general context then narrow down to more specific studies. It's not just a list; it's a story you're telling about what's been explored and what gaps you're aiming to fill. Be clear and concise – your reader should easily follow your line of thought. Make sure to cite your sources properly; that's non-negotiable. Finally, revisions and proofreading can help ensure you have a clear and succinct argument. It's all about presenting a well-organised, thoughtful synthesis of the existing research. You're not just summarising; you're adding your voice to the scholarly conversation. In the textbook *How to Be a Social Worker*, Priscilla Dunk-West (2018, p. 154–155) provides some useful steps for writing and preparing your literature review.

- Group all your articles according to themes. These could be based on anything from the country where the studies originated to the type of method being utilised.
- Take notes as you read. You may like to summarise three key points for each article that you read, especially if you have a large number of articles. If you have printed copies, you might like to use highlighters or sticky notes.
- Begin writing early. Get your ideas down on the page. You can edit and move the text around to make your argument stronger. The key thing is to start writing.
- Avoid summarising the literature. Remember, your role is to critically appraise it.
- Identify the strengths in the other studies and what areas are being neglected.
- Show others your work and ask them to proofread.

Tips for Success

Remember the purpose of your literature review. For example, if you are planning to use a literature review as part of a basis to justify a larger research project, establishing a clear gap in knowledge that lends itself to a viable research project is an essential goal of writing a literature review.

Demonstrate a systematic approach to finding literature by detailing the parameters of your search strategy; for example, the period of time, types of research, sources, keywords, discipline areas, databases, inclusion/exclusion criteria.

Substantiate your claims by ensuring you correctly cite your sources and have citations for any statements or claims made as though they are factual. If you claim a gap in knowledge, you need to be able to substantiate this. Show how you arrived at this observation; don't just tell the reader.

Show your comprehension of the field. Make sure to actually read the article! While it can be tempting just to read the abstract and skip the main content, you don't want the reader to check your claims and discover that you have ignored important findings.

- *Showing understanding of an individual source:* E.g. Smith's (1989) study of _____ showed _____.
- *Showing an understanding of a weakness in an individual study:* Petrov's (1998) study failed to consider _____.

- *Showing understanding of a pattern of knowledge:* Research within the area of _____ is dominated by two basic theoretical positions _____ (statement showing understanding of patterns of knowledge).
- *Showing an understanding of a gap in knowledge:* Whilst there have been several large studies of _____ (Singh, 1999, Ahmadi, 2014, Green, 2015), there has only been one published study concerned with _____(Gray, 2001).

Make your critique convincing; avoid summarising without providing some level of analysis of the information/literature you are presenting. However, a literature review is not an opinion piece, so be wary of making sweeping criticisms without appropriate level of evidence. Don't criticise methodological aspects of a study if you are not confident of your own methodological knowledge, e.g. a qualitative study with a small sample size or a quantitative study which does not produce 'rich' 'insider' data. Make sure that your critique considers both the strengths and limitations and helps to provide a justification for further research or investigation.

Ensure your review is well structured. Start by introducing the topic and its significance. Provide a clear context for your research question and explain why it is important to review the existing literature. Then, present the main themes or theories that emerge from your sources. Critically analyse and compare the findings, methodologies and arguments of different authors. Highlight any gaps or areas for further research.

Revise and edit: Proofread your literature review for clarity, coherence and logical progression of ideas. Ensure that your arguments are well supported by evidence from the sources. Edit for grammar, spelling and formatting errors.

Don't forget to cite your sources! Use proper citation style (e.g. APA, MLA) to give credit to the authors and avoid plagiarism. Create a reference list that includes all the sources you cited in your literature review. Depending on the length of your literature review, you may find it useful to use referencing software such as Endnote.

Student Reflection

My name is Hanna. I am studying a bachelor of social work and currently work in a women's service. The first time I did a literature review was an assignment for a social research method unit at university. I was working as a residential carer in out-of-home care (OOHC) at the time, so I decided to research cultural safety in OOHC within the Australian context. It felt meaningful to me because I was trying to comprehend the whole sector. I thought all social workers eventually have engagement with or need to work within or alongside child protection contexts. I was trying to become informed about the key tensions in the sector and ways to navigate ethical dilemmas. The process of undertaking a literature review was a real turning point for me in terms of my learning; I felt much more confident in my knowledge base and understanding of professional discourse after all those hours of sitting on my bedroom floor, reading papers and highlighting key terms. Through doing a literature review, I learned how to approach information gathering in a systematic way. The process of uncovering new 'knowledge' or ideas is exciting! So too is the idea that you can research anything you want, and the truth (or non-truth) is already out there, and it's up to you what you want to do with that knowledge. I realised that research can be fun and not boring, which is how it was initially presented to me at university. Fortunately, I really engaged with the process, and I discovered that the literature review was like a journey in itself; you go through ridges and valleys, and your feet get sore, but eventually, you will arrive somewhere. There is a possibility that where you arrive is not where you intended to be, but the journey got you there, and so now the question is, will you work the land or carry on? Either way, it's your call as the researcher. I find that empowering.

Conclusion

The literature review serves as a crucial phase in the research process, aiding both the researcher and the reader in understanding established knowledge on a topic. Its goal is to critically analyse existing evidence, identify relationships between sources and lay a solid foundation for one's own research. By addressing gaps and showcasing the relevance of the study, it not only informs but also demonstrates knowledge on contemporary social issues. The chapter outlined various literature types, including peer-reviewed articles, textbooks, edited books, monographs and grey literature. We also explored key processes in the literature-review journey from searching and accessing to ranking and evaluating sources. We maintain that applying a critical lens, which places high value on social justice, is a key ethical consideration in social work research. This critical lens assists us in both critically analysing the research we are reading and to challenge heteronormative, ableist and colonialist assumptions. This chapter also aims to guide readers on initiating, refining and structuring a literature review, encouraging you to take a structured and methodical approach to undertaking a literature review. Remember that the goal of a literature review is not just to summarise or restate what is known but to apply your critical analysis skills to highlight key tensions, debates and gaps in the current landscape. By reading widely and writing regularly, you will avoid the temptation to take shortcuts and, ideally, be able to produce a well-informed, comprehensive and convincing scholarly contribution of your own.

Further Reading

Alston, M., & Bowles, W. (2018). Chapter 6: Systematic reviews. In *Research for social workers: An introduction to methods* (4th ed.). Allen & Unwin.

Aveyard, H., Payne, S., & Preston, N. (2021). *A post-graduate's guide to doing a literature review in health and social care* (2nd ed.). McGraw-Hill Education.

Dekkers, R., Carey, L., & Langhorne, P. (2022). *Making literature reviews work: A multidisciplinary guide to systematic approaches*. Springer. https://doi.org/10.1007/978-3-030-90025-0

Dunk-West, P. (2018). Chapter 7: Research in social work. In *How to be a social worker: A critical guide for students* (2nd ed.). Palgrave Macmillan.

Fink, A. (2019). *Conducting research literature reviews: From the internet to paper*. Sage.

Pan, M. L. (2017). *Preparing literature reviews: Qualitative and quantitative approaches*. Taylor & Francis Group.

References

Choate, P., & Tortorelli, C. (2022). Attachment theory: A barrier for indigenous children involved with child protection. *International Journal of Environmental Research and Public Health*, 19, 8754. https://doi.org/10.3390/ijerph19148754

Crotty, M. (1998). *Foundations of social research: Meaning and perspective in the research process*. Taylor & Francis Group.

Dunk-West, P. (2018). *How to be a social worker: A critical guide for students* (2nd ed.). Palgrave Macmillan.

Lockwood, C., Porritt, K., Munn, Z., Rittenmeyer, L., Salmond, S., Bjerrum, M., Loveday, H., Carrier, J., & Stannard, D. (2020). Chapter 2: Systematic reviews of qualitative evidence. In E. Aromataris & Z. Munn (Eds.), *JBI manual for evidence synthesis*. JBI. https://synthesismanual.jbi.global; https://doi.org/10.46658/JBIMES-20-0

Morley, C., Ablett, P., & Macfarlane, S. (2019). *Engaging with social work: A critical introduction* (2nd ed.). Cambridge University Press.

Morse, J. M. (2015). Data were saturated. . . *Qualitative Health Research, 25*(5), 587–588. https://doi.org/10.1177/1049732315576699

Peters, M. D. J., Godfrey, C., McInerney, P., Munn, Z., Tricco, A. C., & Khalil, H. (2020). Chapter 11: Scoping reviews (2020 version). In E. Aromataris & Z. Munn (Eds.), *JBI manual for evidence synthesis*. JBI. https://synthesismanual.jbi.global; https://doi.org/10.46658/JBIMES-20-12

Rawsthorne, M., Tseris, E., Howard, A., Terare, M., & Sharma, A. (2023). *Using social research for social justice: An introduction for social work and human services* (1st ed.). Routledge.

Ruane, J. M. (2016). *Introducing social research methods: Essentials for getting the edge* (1st ed.). Wiley.

Walters, M. (2019). *Social research methods* (4th ed.). Oxford University Press.

6 Methodology

Chapter Summary

- Methodology outlines a research study's theoretical framework, and ethical considerations and methods are specific techniques used to so-called 'data', or information.
- The elements contained within methodology need to be understood alongside a sound theoretical framework that reflect social work values.
- Research methodologies can be broadly grouped into either quantitative, having a focus on numerical data, or qualitative, which focuses on lived experiences as expressed through language.
- Quantitative research claims to be objective and value free. However, critical social research argues that all research is centred within a value base, and for this reason, social researchers are often drawn to qualitative social research methodologies.
- Key qualitative research methodologies include phenomenology, ethnography, participatory action research, Indigenous methodologies, appreciative inquiry, critical reflection and memory work.

Introduction

The terms 'methodology' and 'methods' are often used interchangeably in social work practice and by those new to learning about research. However, the two terms are indeed distinct, separate and yet equally important aspects of the research design that need to be considered. This chapter hopes to clarify the distinction between methodology and method but also explain to the reader how the two need to work in partnership to ensure a logical, ethical and methodologically sound research project. The elements contained within methodology also need to be understood alongside a sound theoretical framework. Theory, which can often be intimidating to students and practitioners (Morley et al., 2019, p. 162), can be thought of as the lens by which we are understanding and interpreting the world. For this reason, methodology has a strong relationship with your epistemology, a concept which we explored in Chapter 3. This chapter seeks to provide readers with an understanding of the ways in which research ethics (explored in Chapter 4), epistemological positioning, or worldviews, (Chapter 2) and the research question (Chapter 3) work together to lay the foundations for your methodological framework. That is, the overarching view you have of the research topic under investigation, along with the tools with which you plan to engage in your quest to seek answers to your research question, lays your methodological basis. We also present some methodological and theoretical frameworks that are unique to social work and align to the social justice mandate of our profession. Key methodologies that will be explored

DOI: 10.4324/9781003316732-6

include phenomenology, narrative inquiry, memory work, ethnography, critical reflection, Indigenous methodologies and participatory action research.

Method or Methodology?

Methodology and method are two essential elements of our research journey and play an important role in reaching our research aims or destination. Because of the similarity of the way the terms are phrased, sometimes there is confusion about the differences between them. On occasion, people may feel drawn to use them interchangeably; however, they are two separate components of research design and implementation. If we were to take the figurative expression of research being a journey as an example, we could imagine methodology as the car or vehicle driving us to our destination. The car is composed of many separate parts that all need to work in unison and synergy: the engine, the fan belt, the steering wheel, the brakes. This method, then, might be considered the GPS navigation system, or set of maps. It provides a list of steps, e.g. turn left, go straight, cross here; which helps us to arrive at our destination. In theory, if we were to give another person the same map or set of instructions, they should also arrive at the same destination.

In research, our method is just like our map or list of steps that guides us to where we are hoping to go. Methods are the practical, tangible steps we take to collect data, gather evidence, and answer our research questions. They include things such as surveys, interviews, observations, experiments, reflections, content analysis (explored further in Chapter 7). These methods are carefully selected based on the methodology, ensuring that they align with our research objectives and are capable of capturing the nuances of the social research landscape. Just as a skilled driver selects the most appropriate variables (e.g. speed, use of lights, windscreen wipers) for different weather conditions, a researcher selects appropriate methods to reflect their views about the context in which the study is occurring. If the method focuses on the individual steps or processes (the doing), the methodology can be conceptualised as containing the ideas and knowledge required to follow and interpret the steps (the being). It is the implementation of epistemology (knowing).

Narrowing down from epistemology to your method in the research process

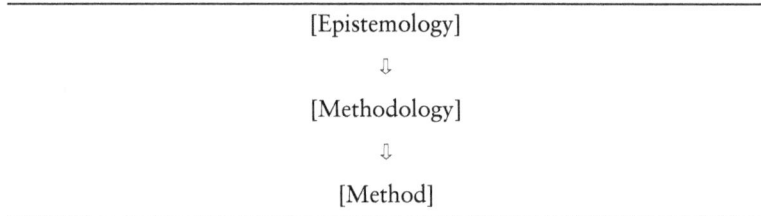

[Epistemology]

⇩

[Methodology]

⇩

[Method]

Quantitative and Qualitative Methodologies

Within social research, research designs tend to fall into the category of either a quantitative or a qualitative methodology. Generally speaking, quantitative research has a focus on numerical and demographic data and an interest in statistical analysis, whereas qualitative research has a focus on narrative and personal accounts drawn from personal stories, spoken word or text. Whether a project is quantitative or qualitative often depends on the nature of the research being investigated and, more specifically, the way in which the research has been understood and interpreted by the researcher (see Chapters 2 and 8).

It is also possible to have an approach to research that falls outside of these two binaries – for example, post-modernist research that would question the validity of any singular construction of 'truth' (Crotty, 2020). However, generally speaking, choosing either a quantitative or qualitative approach will give a researcher enough of a structure and set of parameters on which to base and guide their research design (Sarantakos, 2017).

Quantitative Methodology

Quantitative methodologies stem from a positivist epistemological position, that is, they claim that the nature of reality exists irrespective of human interpretation and thus can be measured through objective means (Creswell & Creswell, 2017). Quantitative methodologies are widely used in health and policy settings to obtain numbers and statistics about key social trends. For example, quantitative data may look at the number of people on public housing lists and then compare these numbers against key demographics such as age, gender and race. Alternatively, quantitative research may be used to measure other social issues such as income disparities between genders or educational disparities among rural and urban settings or make comparisons between health outcomes, incarceration rates or access to resources between different ethnic groups. While quantitative data can reveal an overview of the severity or breadth of an issue, it requires further critical analysis to understand the root causes and driving social forces that influence numerical findings.

Social work has critiqued quantitative methodologies for their claim of being neutral, or value free, because such a position fails to recognise the way in which certain ideas, concepts and knowledges are privileged within society (Alston & Bowles, 2013; Ife, 2012). Having said that, it is important not to discredit the contribution that quantitative methodologies can offer, especially when it comes to studying biomedical issues or scientific issues that rely heavily on mathematical equations (such as geometry, physics, engineering). It is more about recognising that even within these fields, certain views and beliefs and approaches can still be privileged over others, and often, it is at the expense of Indigenous worldviews and understandings (Ife, 2012; Ravulo, 2016). Quantitative research can play a valuable role in shedding light on systemic injustices as long as it is conducted and interpreted with an awareness of social context and power dynamics. Social work does not reject quantitative research outright but rather encourages a critical examination of the assumptions, biases and power dynamics embedded in research methods and the interpretation of data.

Key elements of quantitative research

- Quantitative research is associated with a positivist research paradigm: seeking objective truths.
- Researchers aim to minimise bias using standardised tools to collect numerical data and maintain 'objectivity'.
- There is a strong focus on statistical significance where data is analyzed using statistical techniques.
- Typically, quantitative studies require larger sample sizes to ensure statistical validity.
- Quantitative data collection involves instruments like surveys, experiments and structured observations.
- Quantitative surveys often employs closed-ended questions with fixed response options (e.g. yes/no, like/don't like, agree/disagree).
- Findings are summarised with numerical results, such as means, percentages or correlations. These findings or 'results' are typically presented as numeric data, tables or charts.
- Quantitative research aims to generalise findings to larger population.

Qualitative Methodology

Bloomberg and Volpe (2012, p. 27) suggest that "Qualitative Research is suited to promoting a deep understanding of a social setting or activity as viewed from the perspective of the research participants". Qualitative research is all about diving deep into people's experiences and stories. Instead of relying on numbers, it focuses on open-ended questions and small, carefully chosen groups of participants. Researchers use methods like interviews, self-reflection, memories, observations and analysing text or images to uncover rich, context-specific insights. Unlike quantitative research, which positions the researcher as external and objective to the phenomenon under study, qualitative research locates the researcher within a particular social-cultural-historical setting and encourages a deep analysis of potential bias (Shaw & Gould, 2002; Finlay, 2002). Qualitative approaches value the unique perspectives of individuals and let researchers adapt their methods as key themes and patterns emerge from the study (Holliday, 2007). Along with acknowledging the researchers' own biases, qualitative research aims to shed light on complex social phenomena, often leading to new theories and a better understanding of the human experience. Because of an understanding of lived experience being inherently subjective, context bound and socially influenced, qualitative research tends to be situated within social constructionist or interpretivist paradigms. An example of qualitative research could be in-depth interviews conducted with prisoners in order to gain a better understanding of their experiences of incarceration.

Key elements of qualitative research

- Qualitative methodologies reject a positivist epistemological stance and acknowledge that multiple subjective truths may exist within a single study.
- Qualitative research emphasises exploring subjective experiences and meanings as expressed through language and imagery.
- Qualitative research seeks to understand phenomena with an awareness of broader social-cultural-historical and political contexts.
- Qualitative methods prioritise capturing participants' perspectives and voices and aim for in-depth, rich descriptions of participants' experiences.
- Researchers often use open-ended questions to gather rich, detailed data, and studies may involve smaller, purposive sample sizes.
- Qualitative data is non-numerical and may include textual transcripts, field notes and visual materials that capture people's lived experiences and ideas.
- Ethical qualitative research acknowledges and addresses researcher subjectivity and bias.
- Data analysis involves identifying themes and patterns within the data and often contributes to the development of theory.

Choosing the Right Methodology

If you visualise the methodology as the framework, this means it plays a role in outlining the tone, purpose and goals of your research. Your methodology is important because it helps others reading your research to understand the overall approach, including your philosophical stance and theoretical foundation of the research. The methodology shapes the direction of your study, or research question, and dictates the 'why' and 'how' of your research choices. Because it tells others about what you believe, what you value and how you understand the nature of the world, methodology also considers questions of ethics (see Chapter 4). Our commitment to ethical research as social workers is core to our value base. In writing your methodology, it's important that you can show the clear link between what is considered of value in social work and how this is represented in your research actions. Together your method and methodology represent a dynamic relationship that ensures research rigour, ethical integrity and the ability to generate meaningful insights into the complex fabric of society.

Another way to conceptualise methodology is to imagine it as your research 'recipe'; this includes the key ingredients you will later utilise as you apply your methods, or steps you take in your research process. The key ingredients that make up your methodology are your epistemology, or worldview, that we explored in Chapter 2, as well as your social work theories. Epistemology helps us to understand the nature of the world around us, and theory helps us to explain and interpret what we are seeing. It is the way we construct our view of reality. Both your epistemology and methodology reflect your beliefs and values and play a role in how we design research. For example, let's consider the topic that relates to the sexual health and well-being of young people. If you have a positivist epistemological positioning, you view reality as objective and independent from conscious experience. From a positivist view, humans are rational beings governed by certain social and natural, observable laws. These laws and empirically observable processes cause predictable outcomes that, when reproduced, produce consistent results (Sarantakos, 2017). For this reason, a positivist researcher may assume that if sexual health education is delivered consistently to young people, then there will be a decline in the rates of sexually transmitted diseases (based on the empirical link between sexual health education and lower rates of disease). A positivist researcher may choose a quantitative methodology to measure rates of sexually transmitted diseases among young people before the education program and then at periods of time following the conclusion of the program. This could be done using a survey and/or by reviewing rates of sexually transmitted diseases in the community. This research is considered quantitative in methodology, because it has a focus on *quantifying* the problem through numerical or statistical means. These numbers are considered objective and value neutral.

Example Quantitative Research Design

Topic:	Young People and Sexual Health
Epistemology:	Positivist
Aims:	To review the effectiveness of school-based sex education programs in reducing the rates of sexually transmitted disease among young people aged 12–17 years
Example Research Question:	Do rates of sexually transmitted diseases decrease among young people who have participated in school-based sexual education programs?
Methodology	Quantitative
Methods	Individual online health survey to measure the rates of sexually transmitted diseases among young people prior to their commencement of the sexual education course and 6 months following the completion

Conversely, a qualitative researcher might opt for a social constructionist approach to understand the experiences of young people participating in a sexual health education program. Because social constructionism acknowledges that the participants' voices and interpretations are essential in constructing a holistic understanding of the issue, they could use methods such as in-depth interviews or focus group discussions to gather rich, narrative data from the participants. By listening to their stories and examining the nuances in their experiences, the researcher aims to uncover the multifaceted impact of the program on their lives. This research is considered qualitative because it seeks to explore the subjective perspectives and meanings attributed to the program's effects rather than quantifying outcomes numerically. This approach is all about understanding the personal stories and meanings behind the program's impact rather than just counting numbers. It's like seeing the bigger picture through the eyes and words of the people involved. And unlike the just the facts style of quantitative research, qualitative research values the diverse perspectives and personal interpretations that add depth to the story.

Example Qualitative Research Design

Topic:	Young People and Sexual Health
Epistemology:	Social constructionist
Aims:	To reduce rates of sexually transmitted diseases among young people by understanding the barriers to accessing and enacting safe sex
Example Research Question:	What are the barriers to sexual health among young people aged 12–17?
Methodology	Qualitative
Methods	Individual interviews with young people who have participated in a school-based sexual education program in the past 6 months

Indigenous Methodologies

Historically, social research (read Western research) has been slow to accept the value of Indigenous worldviews because of their apparent lack of 'scientific knowledge' (Faleolo, 2013). Both social and hard sciences have maintained the idea of expert social researchers and thus have often rejected the idea that local people, untrained in the theories and methods of conventional social science, can make valuable contributions to both the form and the substance of a social research process (Smith, 2021). Sadly, this privileging of Western epistemological thought contributes to a cross-cultural research context in which the Western researcher examines the experience of non-Western participants (Farrelly & Nabobo-Baba, 2014; Tamasese et al., 2005). Such an approach fails to appreciate the nuances of the local context and produce research that is meaningful, appropriate and culturally viable for non-Western community contexts (Vaka et al., 2016). Therefore, research strategies that seek to understand and interpret data by drawing on indigenous constructs and local knowledge bases are vital (Ravulo, 2016; Vaka et al., 2016; Farrelly & Nabobo-Baba, 2014; Tamasese et al., 2005). However, when engaging in research methodologies that seek to capitalise on Indigenous epistemologies, non-Indigenous researchers need to be wary of processes whereby Indigenous methods become culturally appropriated by non-Indigenous researchers in an effort to legitimise their own research process. Thus, we encourage anyone considering the use of Indigenous methodologies by one who doesn't identify as belonging to that community, to exercise caution and to ask themselves, "Am I really the best person to be doing this research?"

Our intention in encouraging readers to exercise caution with regards to Indigenous methodologies is neither to discourage people from engaging in cross-cultural research nor to shut down conversations about Indigenous epistemological beliefs and practices. Instead, it is to promote a decolonising agenda that highlights the way in which First Nations voices have been marginalised, discredited and systematically prevented from engaging in research processes (Geia et al., 2013). There is also a long tradition of being researched 'on', despite the fact that very few health, economic or social benefits have been realised by Indigenous groups, particularly in situations in which colonial rule is still the dominant form of political process (Bennett, 2020). Drawing from First Nations epistemologies and practice offers researchers a rich tapestry of ideas by which to develop understandings of the world and the ways in which human experience can be understood. Meo-Sewabu (2014), when reflecting on her experiences as a Fijian woman engaging in research in the Aotearoa: New Zealand context, suggests that research which borrows from the world-views of both Indigenous and Western epistemologies can be woven together to create a strong tapestry of understanding and collective knowledge. Certainly, any research methodology that has clear alignment with the cultural and worldviews of participants should be given due weight in the consideration of methodological choices in the research design process (Rowe et al., 2015).

Critical, anti-oppressive and decolonising research paradigms all call for Western hegemony within social research processes to be challenged (Briskman, 2014). To this end, Indigenous methodologies represent unique ways of understanding social phenomena in ways that are applicable and relevant to the local context (Smith, 2021). However, if social work practice and research is to uphold a commitment to decolonising practices, it is important to not only promote Indigenous methodologies but also ensure that the roadblocks to enacting Indigenous-led research are addressed. This means ensuring First Nations communities and individuals are given opportunities to lead the research process and to participate and contribute to conversations as to the nature of research within the academy (Bennett, 2020). Most notably, it also means that non-Indigenous researchers may need to step aside from roles which see them as driving the researcher process to those in which they become critical allies in decolonisation efforts within research.

Qualitative Approaches in Social Work Research

A defining attribute of qualitative research is its adaptability (Shaw & Holland, 2014). Researchers can tailor their approach to the unique context of the people they are working with, and unlike the rigidity of quantitative designs, qualitative methodologies can accommodate the evolving nature of the inquiry. Social work and the social sciences frequently favour qualitative research methodologies due to their epistemological alignment with the values of social justice, equity and honouring lived experiences (Rawsthorne et al., 2024). Qualitative research is characterised by its capacity to delve deeply into the complexities of human experiences and phenomena, offering a comprehensive understanding that attempts to centre participants' voices. It also offers an opportunity for the researcher to name their positionality and recognise power dynamics in the construction, implementation and dissemination of research. By challenging traditional research paradigms, qualitative methodologies also contribute to expanding the body of knowledge in social work and social sciences, offering alternative perspectives and frameworks. Given the suitability of qualitative methodologies within social work research, a number of key approaches are presented in what follows. This is by no means an exhaustive list but rather offers a starting point for reflection and inquiry. A list of suggested further readings is offered at the conclusion of this chapter.

Phenomenology

Phenomenology is a qualitative research approach that centres on examining an individual's firsthand and lived experiences. As a methodology, it is uniquely positioned to provide social workers an opportunity to learn from the experiences of others (Neubauer et al., 2019). Engelland (2020) suggests that if biology is the study of life (*bios*), then phenomenology is the study of appearance (*phenomena*), quite literally taken from the Greek *phainomenon*, meaning 'that which appears'. Generally, a phenomenon is anything that can be experienced in some sort of way (Williams, 2021). So we can understand phenomenology as the study of lived experience, and this can be either descriptive or interpretive in nature (Matua & Van Der Wal, 2015).

Given that there are many different philosophies that inform social work practice, it is not surprising that there is a broad set of phenomenological traditions from which a researcher can draw. To choose a phenomenological research methodology requires the researcher to reflect on the values and epistemological position they represent (Neubauer et al., 2019). Following is a summary of the way in which different epistemological positions influence the phenomenological approach to research. When deciding on which way to approach a phenomenological study, it is vital that there is a clear and consistent alignment between the epistemological position of the research (Chapter 2), the research question (Chapter 3) and the methodology.

Key Components of Descriptive and Interpretive Phenomenology (adapted from Neubauer et al., 2019, p. 92)

Descriptive Phenomenology	*Interpretive Phenomenology*
Ontological assumptions: Reality is internal to the knower; what appears in their consciousness Epistemological assumptions: Observer must separate him/herself from the world, including his/her own physical being, to reach the state of the transcendental; bias-free; understands phenomena by descriptive means Role of researcher: Consider phenomena from different perspectives, identify units of meaning and cluster into themes to form textural description (the 'what' of the phenomenon). Use imaginative variation to create structural (the how) description. Combine these descriptions to form the essence of the phenomenon.	Ontological assumptions: Lived experience is an interpretive process situated in an individual's lifeworld Epistemological assumptions: Observer is part of the world and not bias free; understands phenomenon by interpretive means Role of researcher: Reflects on essential themes of participant experience with the phenomenon while simultaneously reflecting on the researcher's own experience. Iterative cycles of capturing and writing reflections towards a robust and nuanced analysis; consider how the data (or parts) contributed to evolving understanding of the phenomenon (whole).

In phenomenological research, the job of the researcher is to understand what the person being studied is feeling and thinking deep inside themselves. Building trust is of paramount importance because it helps the person feel safe to share their thoughts and experiences openly. There are often long, unstructured interviews, which can last an hour or even more. The theory is that long interviews give the person enough time to talk about what really matters to them and helps the researcher make sure they're really hearing what the person wants to say. These conversations are often recorded before being transcribed and analysed (Denscombe, 2010). Another key element of phenomenology is asking the researcher to undertake what is known as bracketing, which is where the researcher identifies their own ideas and bias with the goal of then being able to set these aside in the data analysis process. A key criticism of phenomenology is the inherently biased nature of all interpretive processes, and the influence of self in the research process is something that of which any researcher utilising phenomenology needs to be aware (Hayes, 2000).

Strengths and Limitations of Phenomenology

- Phenomenology allows researchers to explore how people perceive an event or phenomenon rather than simply how the phenomenon impacts or manifests free of the interpretations of individuals and communities.
- Phenomenology is suited to small-scale research because it is reliant on in-depth interviews which can be undertaken in specific localities, such as hospitals, schools or organisations, and when funding is limited and the researcher is the main resource.
- For those who are not familiar with its philosophical underpinnings or methodological application, phenomenology can seem challenging to apply to social research contexts.
- Like other qualitative methods, law- and policymakers may not give phenomenological studies as much credibility as 'empirical' studies.
- It may not be possible for us to entirely suspend our presuppositions when considering the views and opinions of other people, and for this reason, there is argument over whether the results are 'reliable'.

Ethnography

Ethnography is a methodology that draws from a number of different traditions, namely constructionism, phenomenology and hermeneutics. It is a methodology widely associated with anthropology, which is a discipline which aims to study human societies, cultures and their development (Bradford & Cullen, 2013). There have been many instances of anthropologists travelling to other countries in order to study the cultures that live there (Seremetakis, 2017). Most notably, this has occurred in a one-way transfer in which Anglo researchers would travel to 'exotic' lands to watch and observe cultures and then make inferences as to the meanings of behaviour and cultural practice. This has raised criticism in post-colonial contexts because the transfer of knowledge is often for the benefit of the researcher, and ultimately, the researcher controls the narrative because events and observations are still interpreted through a Western lens (McCall, 2011).

In ethnographic methodology, immersion in the field is considered the test of validity: it allows the researcher to obtain what is known as an 'emic', or insider, point of view (Walter, 2019). It also involves observing, recording and writing about your observations to enable what is known as *thick description* (Walters, 1980). Often, this involves a combination of methods such as interviews, systematic observations, field notes and personal accounts, visual documenting and recording. These methods may follow a formal and structured design such as individual interviews, or they may be more organic and fluid, such as the unstructured conversations that may happen with people as part of day-to-day being in the field (Wiles et al., 2008). In recent years, the use of technology and visual methods has also become a strong feature of ethnography (Natasi, 2013; Bradford & Cullen, 2013). Although there is nothing inherently different in the methodological design of visual ethnography to that of more written approaches, it is important that deep consideration of ethical consequences take place prior to engaging in research.

For example, the use of photographs is considered socially taboo in some cultures, especially if these are of people who have died or those of sacred sites. The use of images of children, as well as photographs of people who may be involved in activities such as drug use or sex work, may also bring about negative consequences for the subjects from having their images publically displayed. For more on ethics in research, please review Chapter 4.

Strengths and Limitations of Ethnography

- Ethnography provides an immersive research experience in which the researcher takes an active and hands-on role in participating in the community in which the research is occurring. In this way, the research is said to be organic, allowing for multiple sources of information and observations to be gathered.
- Ethnography combines many methods including semi-structured interviews, participant observations, field notes, visual documentation and recordings. The mixed-method approach enables the researcher to obtain a thorough picture of the research context.
- Data 'findings' are generated through an authentic setting rather than being constructed or artificially staged.
- The time taken to build relationships, nurture relationships and document experiences is considerable. An ethnographic approach requires a significant time commitment and genuine desire to maintain community relationships.
- The ethnographer plays a key role in interpreting the world through their own cultural lens; without an awareness of positionality, there is a risk of cultural stereotyping and misinterpretation.
- The interpretation of events and language used can reflect the dominant ideology of the ethnographer as well as dominant social theories and discourses. Critical analysis and reflexivity on the part of the researcher are required to ensure culturally and ethically sound research processes.

Critical Reflection

As a research methodology, critical reflection is of increasing interest to social work because of its capabilities in naming and identifying the way in which our lived understandings entwine with dominant discourse. It connects individual experiences to broader social structures and becomes a political act in the sense that connections between social-political context and shared manifestations of oppression can be identified (Pease, 2020). Stemming from the work of Schön (1983, 1987), who pioneered a model of professional reflection within education, critical reflection shares disciplinary influence from education and other social sciences. Schön (1983) challenged the idea that knowledge from systematic research alone should guide practice, emphasising that theory is implicit in our actions and often diverges from our stated beliefs. Mezirow (1991) and Brookfield (1991) then built on the work of Schön by highlighting critical reflection's role in questioning underlying beliefs and assumptions, encouraging a deeper understanding of why we do what we do. They argue that the deliberate reflective process of examining presuppositions and assumptions promotes more effective, self-aware practitioners who bridge the gap between theory and practice.

Perhaps the most well-known and accepted model of critical reflection is encapsulated in the work of Jan Fook (1993, 2008, 2016). Fook's deconstruction-reconstruction model of critical reflection is a structured approach that guides individuals in critically examining their own beliefs, assumptions, and experiences. It involves two main phases:

1 Deconstruction: In this phase, individuals break down their existing thoughts, beliefs and assumptions. They question and challenge these perspectives, exploring where

they come from and how they might be influenced by societal norms, culture or personal experiences. Deconstruction encourages self-awareness and the identification of biases or preconceptions that may impact one's understanding of a situation or issue.

2 Reconstruction: Following the deconstruction phase, individuals work on reconstructing their beliefs and assumptions in a more informed and critical manner. They integrate new insights gained from the deconstruction process and consider alternative viewpoints. Reconstruction fosters a deeper understanding of complex issues and encourages the development of more inclusive, ethical and socially just perspectives.

As a research methodology, the appeal of critical reflection is the overt manner in which research production, dissemination and consumption are acknowledged as socially constructed and subjective. In recognising the researcher's role in the creation and reproduction of knowledge, there is acknowledgement of the ways in which interpreting and consequential re-telling of knowledge is an inherently political process (Morley, 2015). For critical reflection to maintain validity as a research methodology, it is important that it follows a deliberate process. Although there are many models of (non-critical) reflection, including those used in participatory action research, for reflection to be 'critical', there needs to be alignment with critical theory. Critical theory is an approach to understanding society that actively names, reveals and critiques power and the way in which this manifests in social structures such as gender or social class (Morley et al., 2019). This means that when using critical reflection as a methodology, there is a deliberate process by which the researcher seeks to connect lived experience to broader social-political and cultural influences. This is the main delineation from ethnography, which may document lived experiences but does not place the same demands on the researcher to name their positionality and consider how dominant discourses have shaped their experiences.

Strengths and Limitations of Critical Reflection

- Critical reflective research encourages the researcher to actively name their positionality and potential bias in the research process, rejecting objectivist and positivist epistemological positioning as paradigms that privilege heteronormativity and Eurocentrism.
- As a methodology, critical reflection is low cost because it does not rely on special instruments or resources in which to enact the process; the researchers themselves are the primary instruments in critical research methodology.
- Critical reflection promotes ethical and culturally responsive research by ensuring that researchers are aware of and name personal bias, power differentials and potential ethical dilemmas in their research.
- Critical reflection as a methodology is a new and emerging field. This can make it difficult to find resources and models by which to build a case when using critical reflection as a tool in a PhD dissertation or defence.
- Critical reflection, although widely accepted as a legitimate tool and process within social work, struggles to find methodological recognition within the so called main line sciences.

Narrative Inquiry

Originally developed by Connelly and Clandinin (1990) to explore the personal experiences of teachers, narrative inquiry has become a methodology widely used across education, anthropology and social science disciplines (Butina, 2015). It is a form of research in which participants provide the researcher with their life experiences through thick, rich stories. The stories themselves then become the raw data (Bleakley, 2005). Examples of inquiries that yield narrative data include interviews that solicit stories, written autobiographies, letters, biographies or oral histories (Connelly & Clandinin, 1990).

In developing their methodology, Connelly and Clandinin (1990, p. 4) stress that *in beginning the process of narrative inquiry, it is particularly important that all participants have a voice within the relationship*. Typically, entering a research setting is seen as an ethical responsibility incumbent upon the researcher. However, within research inquiry, ethical responsibility is seen as a negotiated process because the research process involves building relationships in which experiences are shared. Narrative inquiry in this context happens within these researcher–practitioner relationships, forming a caring community. For research participants who may have felt voiceless in research, this can be a challenge, but creating a caring community through dialogue and modelling can promote an empowering and transformative experience (Teng, 2020). Similar to many of the qualitative methods presented in this book, it is not only attractive to social work research because of the way in which lived experience is valued but also the collaborative approach to working and research 'with' rather than 'on' individuals and communities (Saxton, 2018, 2021). It is a popular methodology in qualitative research because of the capacity to reveal unique perspectives, often from marginalised or silenced groups, and enable deeper understanding of a situation (Clandinin, 2019).

Strengths and Limitations of Narrative Inquiry

- Narrative inquiry places ethical considerations at the forefront, ensuring that participants' rights and well-being are respected throughout the research process.
- Narrative inquiry allows for a deep exploration of individuals' stories and experiences, providing an in-depth understanding of their lives and challenges.
- In narrative inquiry, the story is seen as a valid form of raw data. This has wide inter-cultural and cross-disciplinary application because it provides an avenue to record and document oral histories. Until recently, oral cultural knowledge has often been discredited or disregarded by conventional sciences because of the assumption that these knowledge bases lack empirical rigour. Narrative inquiry honours and values storytelling.
- True to the values of social work, narrative inquiry and research can serve as powerful tools for advocacy, amplifying the voices of marginalised individuals and advocating for social change.
- The researcher must be heavily engaged with the research topic and have a deep connection and relationship with participants in order to effectively and realistically represent their life experiences.
- The extensive volume of data to be processed in narrative research can be time intensive, extending beyond the interview phase itself, and requires significant resourcing and investment.
- Stories and cultural knowledge run the risk of being commodified or appropriated by Western research paradigms.

Memory Work

Developed by German sociologist Fridda Haug (1987), the focus in memory work is acknowledging and valuing lived experience and considering memories as a valid form of raw data. In Haug's original approach (1987), the method of memory work follows specific guidelines in which researchers move through three distinct stages of writing and rewriting their experiences. In the first stage, researchers write their memories of a lived experience in third person. The idea behind writing in the third person is to create space and distance for the emotional and sensory to emerge (Bryant & Bryant, 2019). After this, researchers can move into the second stage, in which the written memories are shared with the collective, who then work collaboratively to develop shared meaning and understanding (Crawford et al., 1992). This collective analysis aims to uncover the common social understanding of each event, the social meanings embodied in the actions described in the written accounts and how these meanings are arrived. In the final stage, these 'findings' are further theorised and examined alongside dominant understandings and social constructions to uncover the way in which social forces may have influenced shared and collective experiences. In this way, the third phase seeks to actively contribute to theory development and link lived experience to the broader social-political experience (Haug, 1987).

Since Haug's original methodological design, memory work has been influenced by other theoretical traditions such as phenomenology, hermeneutics, post-modernism and symbolic interactionism. Haug's intention was that the stages and process of memory work remain flexible and adaptable, and therefore, memory work has been adapted in various ways. Memory work is more than just journalling or self-observation; it is a recognised social science methodology in which researchers engage in a deliberate process of writing in the third person and time for analysis and rewriting (Bryant & Bryant, 2019). Although first developed as a collective method, over time, memory work has also been used as collective autoethnography (Newcomb et al., 2023; Bryant & Livholts, 2013) and with individual participants (Onyx & Small, 2001). Irrespective of whether memory work is a collective or individual process, the focus of memory work is not autobiographical in the sense of constructing a public account of self and self-experience but rather a theoretical, feminist and sociological process in which experience is deconstructed (Lapadat et al., 2010).

Strengths and Limitations of Memory Work

- Memory work and feminist methodologies challenge assumptions that position research as objective and rather advocate for transparency in acknowledging the researcher's standpoint and potential biases. As such, there is an emphasis on power dynamics within research, promoting ethical research practices and reflexivity among researchers.
- Feminist methodologies such a memory work recognise the interconnectedness of various social identities (e.g. gender, race, class, sexuality) and how they intersect to shape individuals' experiences, leading to a more inclusive and nuanced analysis.
- In memory work, the voices of marginalised groups, including women and LGBTQ+ individuals who have often been underrepresented or excluded in traditional research, are amplified.
- As an established and recognised qualitative method, memory work allows for comprehensive exploration of personal narratives and experiences, enriching the research with context and depth.
- For some, the process of sharing memories can be empowering; however, the process can also be emotionally demanding for both researchers and participants.
- The fluidity of this methodology is often critiqued by those within the positivist traditions, and thus the validity of this methodology is undermined, particularly by the 'hard' sciences. This can make it challenging when trying to obtain ethics clearance, funding or scholarship when many university and research committees remain rooted in objectivist and patriarchal paradigms.

Participatory Action Research

Traditionally, action research (AR) is characterised as a dynamic process of experiential learning and knowledge acquisition in which research and practice are tightly interwoven (Crane & O'Regan, 2010). There is a focus on research resulting in tangible and practical changes (or action), which is then reviewed, evaluated, refined and again reviewed in an iterative process (Chevalier & Buckles, 2019). Stemming from the work of Paulo Freire and the goals for social emancipation, participatory action research adds to the reflective and transformational goals of AR to focus on the views of participants, who are viewed as active co-contributors to knowledge (Rauch et al., 2014). Participatory action research (PAR) places significant emphasis on the active involvement of individuals affected by the research topic. It offers an avenue to transcend passive roles within the research process, positioning participants as equitable co-researchers (Fine & Torre, 2021). This approach is pivotal in addressing power imbalances, affording individuals the agency to participate in and shape all facets of the research, from methodological choices to the application of research outcomes.

PAR relies on relationships between the researcher and the participants; in essence, all participants are equal co-participants. In reality, research is often funded or structured such that positions of hierarchy exist within organisational and community structures that may not be acknowledged under the guise of the research being 'participatory'. This also applies to diverse cultural contexts in which social hierarchies exist within the community, so the views of the majority may serve to reflect the views of those with the most power. This relies on skilled facilitation, critical reflection and robust relationship building (Alston & Bowles, 2013). Furthermore, despite PAR being ideological rooted in the goals of social justice and emancipatory change, researchers who are coming into community or organisational contexts to facilitate PAR should recognise that the burden of risk is not shared equally when it comes to challenging social injustice (Saxton, 2018). In some contexts, social advocacy can even present a risk of social or physical harm for participants. Ideally, PAR is conducted by group members as a collective process to a collectively identified issue rather than being a process that is imposed by a researcher outside of the collective.

Strengths and Limitations of PAR

- PAR values lived experience and tacit knowledge, seeing participants as co-contributors to the research process and rejecting the expert positionality of the researcher. In this way, the focus moves away from researching 'on' to researching 'with'.
- PAR is rooted in ethical research principles, emphasising informed consent, participant well-being and the ethical treatment of sensitive topics. This ensures that the research process is conducted with integrity and respect.
- PAR often involves collaboration between researchers and participants from various disciplines, fostering a multidimensional understanding of complex issues. It is also adaptable and reflexive, allowing for change and adjustments throughout the research process.
- PAR generates contextually rich insights by drawing on the lived experiences and local knowledge of participants. This approach results in research outcomes that are highly relevant to the specific community or context under study.
- The process of relationship and trust building takes time, particularly in contexts in which communities have been exploited or trust has been broken between researchers or those perceived to be outside the community and the insider community members.
- Often, funding bodies or university requirements are such that imposed timelines detract from the capacity to develop deep and reciprocal relationships.

Grounded Theory

Grounded theory was developed as a methodology by Barney Glaser and Anselm Strauss in the mid-1960s in an effort to move away from the traditional social sciences research model, which aimed to test existing theories (Bryant & Charmaz, 2012, 2019). Since the publication of Glaser and Strauss's (1967) seminal text, *The Discovery of Grounded Theory*, grounded theory has evolved to be a globally recognised and valued approach to social research. As the name suggests, it is an approach to research that aims to generate theory that is grounded in data (Birks & Mills, 2022). Essentially, it aims to understand why and how events happen as well as why people behave in specific ways. By closely observing a population, a researcher employing the grounded theory approach can construct a theory that explains the phenomena under investigation (Tenny et al., 2022).

Kathy Charmaz, who was a former student of Glaser and Strauss, made a significant contribution to Grounded Theory methodology. Unlike the initial positioning of researchers as distant experts, Charmaz (2006, 2014) emphasised that researchers are actively involved in the research process, co-constructing experiences and meanings with participants. Charmaz introduced the term 'constructivist grounded theory', highlighting that researchers should focus on understanding what and how phenomena are studied. Social constructionist grounded theorists argue that data and its analysis should be understood within the context of the participants' situation (Charmaz, 2014). Successfully engaging with grounded theory also requires a willingness to be reflexive and clearly engage with your positionality (Birks et al., 2019). The willingness to question and challenge the expert position of the researcher has strong alignment with social work values, which also seek to challenge the privilege and professional status and simultaneously promote diverse lived experiences and ways of knowing.

Strengths and Limitations of Grounded Theory

- Grounded theory's inductive approach allows flexibility in exploring and generating theories directly from data, avoiding rigid preconceptions of what the data should say. The bottom-up process enables a more organic development of concepts, allowing them to emerge from the data rather than being imposed from existing theories.
- The methodology accommodates teamwork, encouraging collaboration in coding and analysis, which can enhance the rigour and depth of the research.
- The evolution of grounded theory, particularly with Charmaz's constructivist approach, recognises the active role of researchers in co-constructing meaning with participants, fostering a deeper connection to the studied context. The emphasis on reflexivity further aligns with social work values, encouraging researchers to critically examine their own positionality and challenge traditional power dynamics in research.
- Despite the focus on reflexivity and the recognition of the role of the researcher, there is still the risk of misinterpretation of the results, particularly if coding is done in isolation.
- Grounded theory has traditionally been viewed as time-consuming, potentially limiting its feasibility for researchers with tight timelines or resource constraints.
- The success of grounded theory is heavily dependent on the skills, reflexivity and theoretical understanding of the researcher. Additionally, the constant comparative method and iterative coding process can be intellectually demanding, requiring a high level of analytical skills and expertise, which may be a barrier for novice researchers.

Conclusion

Methodology and method are fundamental components of the research process, often causing confusion due to their similar phrasing. While they may appear interchangeable, they are distinct elements of research design and execution. Methods encompass concrete steps for data collection, such as surveys, interviews, observations and experiments carefully chosen to align with the research objectives and capture the social research landscape's nuances (more on this in Chapter 7). The methodology on the other hand, acts as the overarching framework, shaping the researcher's worldview, theoretical foundation and ethical considerations. In this chapter, we identified two key streams within methodological design; this includes quantitative methodologies, which focus on statistical analysis and numerical data, and qualitative methodologies, which have more of a focus on narrative and lived experience. Because of social work's alignment to social constructionism and practises that privilege the voices of the marginalised, a number of qualitative methodological examples were also examined. These explorations of phenomenology, narrative inquiry, ethnography, critical reflection, memory work and PAR serve as an introduction to diverse methodological frameworks. It is important to highlight that for each of these methodological constructs, a book in and of itself could (and has) been written. This chapter provides an introductory overview to key methodological approaches that align with the social justice mandate of social work and is a great starting point for anyone embarking on a research journey. It is envisioned that the suggested reading list, along with the researcher's own further investigation, will be utilised when drawing on this text to develop your own research design.

This chapter also celebrates the contribution of Indigenous knowledges in understanding how best to care for the environment and society. We also acknowledge the ways in which Indigenous worldviews have been systematically marginalised and devalued within mainstream research paradigms that privilege Western scientific thought and position the researcher as 'expert'. Aligning with a diverse range of qualitative approaches that value narrative and an ideological view that each individual and community are experts in their own lives, this chapter encourages non-Indigenous researchers to ensure their research acts in allyship rather than competition with community. This applies to any research methodology presented in this chapter. The goal is not to discourage cross-cultural research but to highlight the need for community-led and participant voices to play a central role in research design and dissemination.

Further Reading

Bloustein, G. (2003). *Girl making: A cross-cultural Ethnography on the process of growing up female*. Berghan Books.

Bryant, L., & Bryant, K. (2019). Memory work. In P. Liamputtong (Ed.), *Handbook of research methods in health social sciences* (pp. 527–540). Springer.

Charmaz, K. (2014). *Constructing grounded theory*. Sage.

Connelly, F. M., & Clandinin, D. J. (1990). Stories of experience and narrative inquiry. *Educational Researcher, 19*(5), 2–14. https://doi.org/10.2307/1176100

Creswell, J. (2013). *Qualitative inquiry and research design: Choosing among five approaches.* (3rd ed.). Sage.

Fraser, H., & Michell, D. (2015). Feminist memory work in action: Method and practicalities. *Qualitative Social Work, 14*(3), 321–337. https://doi.org/10.1177/1473325014539374

Glaser, B., & Strauss, A. (2017). *Discovery of grounded theory: Strategies for qualitative research.* Routledge.

Glaser, B. G. (2006). *Doing formal grounded theory: A proposal*. Sociology Press.

Kemmis, S., McTaggart, R., & Nixon, R. (2014). *The action research planner: Doing critical participatory action research*. Springer.

Liamputtong, P. (2020). *Qualitative research methods*. Oxford University Press.

Neubauer, B. E., Witkop, C. T., & Varpio, L. (2019). How phenomenology can help us learn from the experiences of others. *Perspectives on Medical Education, 8*, 90–97. https://doi.org/10.1007/s40037-019-0509-2

O'Toole, J. (2018). Institutional storytelling and personal narratives: Reflecting on the value of narrative inquiry. *Institutional Educational Studies, 37*(2), 175–189. https://doi.org/10.1080/03 323315.2018.1465839

Tatano Beck, C. (2020). *Introduction to phenomenology: Focus on methodology.* Sage.

References

Alston, M., & Bowles, W. (2013). *Research for social workers: An introduction to methods* (3rd ed.). Routledge.

Back, L. (1996). *New ethnicities and urban culture: Racism and multiculture in young lives.* Routledge.

Back, L. (2007). *The art of listening.* Berg.

Bennett, B. (2020). Acknowledgements in Aboriginal social work research: How to counteract neo-liberal academic complacency. In S. M. Tascon & J. Ife (Eds.), *Disrupting whiteness in social work.* Routledge/Taylor and Francis Group.

Birks., M., Hoare, K., & Mills, J. (2019). Grounded theory: The FAQs. *International Journal of Qualitative Methods, 18.* p 1–7. https://doi.org/10.1177/160940619882535

Birks, M., & Mills, J. (2022). *Grounded theory: A practical guide.* Sage.

Bleakley, A. (2005). Stories as data, data as stories: Making sense of narrative inquiry in clinical education. *Medical Education, 39,* 534–540.

Bloomberg, L. D., & Volpe, M. (2012). *Completing your qualitative dissertation: A road map from beginning to end.* Sage Publications.

Bradford, S., & Cullen, F. (Eds.). (2013). *Research and research methods for youth practitioners.* Routledge.

Briskman, L. (2014). *Social work with indigenous communities: A human rights approach* (2nd ed.). Federation Press.

Brookfield, S. (1991). Using critical incidents to explore learners' assumptions. In J. Mezirow & Associates (Eds.), *Fostering critical reflection in adulthood. A guide to transformative and emancipatory learning.* Jossey-Bass.

Bryant, A., & Charmaz, K. (2012). Grounded theory and psychological research. In H. Cooper, P. M. Camic, D. L. Long, A. T. Panter, D. Rindskopf & K. J. Sher (Eds.), *APA handbook of research methods in psychology* (Vol. 2, pp. 39–56). American Psychological Association.

Bryant, A., & Charmaz, C. (2012, 2019). *The Sage handbook of current developments in grounded theory.* Sage Publications Ltd.

Bryant, L., & Bryant, K. (2019). Memory work. In P. Liamputtong (Ed.), *Handbook of research methods in health social sciences* (pp. 527–540). Springer.

Bryant, L., & Livholts, M. (2013). Location and unlocation: Examining gender and telephony through autoethnographic textual and visual methods. *The International Journal of Qualitative Methods, 12,* 403–419.

Butina, M. (2015). A narrative approach to qualitative inquiry. *American Society for Clinical Laboratory Science, 28*(3), 190–196. https://doi.org/10.29074/ascls.28.3.190

Charmaz, K. (2006). *Constructing grounded theory: A practical guide through qualitative analysis.* Sage.

Charmaz, K. (2014). *Constructing grounded theory.* Sage.

Chevalier, J. M., & Buckles, D. J. (2019). *Participatory action research: Theory and methods for engaged inquiry* (2nd ed.). Routledge. https://doi.org/10.4324/9781351033268

Clandinin, D. J. (2019). *Journeys in narrative inquiry: The selected works of D. Jean Clandinin.* Routledge.

Connelly, F. M., & Clandinin, D. J. (1990). Stories of experience and narrative inquiry. *Educational Researcher, 19*(5), 2–14. https://doi.org/10.2307/1176100

Crane, P., & O'Regan, M. (2010). *On PAR: Using participatory action research to improve early intervention.* Department of Families, Housing, Community Services and Indigenous Affairs, Australian Government.

Crawford, J., Kippax, S., Onyx, J., Gault, U., & Benton, P. (1992). *Emotion and gender: Constructing meaning from memory.* Newbury Park.

Creswell, J. W., & Creswell, J. D. (2017). *Research design: Qualitative, quantitative, and mixed methods approaches* (5th ed.). SAGE Publications, Inc. https://bookshelf.vitalsource.com/books/9781506386690

Crotty, M. (2020). *The foundations of social research: Meaning and perspective in the research process*. Routledge, Taylor & Francis Group.

Denscombe, M. (2010). *The good research guide for small-scale social research projects* (3rd ed.). McGraw-Hill Education.

Engelland, C. (2020). *Phenomenology*. The MIT Press.

Faleolo, M. (2013). Authentication in social work education: The balancing act. In C. Noble, M. Hendrickson & I. Y. Han (Eds.), *Social work education: Voices from the Asia Pacific* (2nd ed.). University of Sydney Press.

Farrelly, T., & Nabobo-Baba, U. (2014). Talanoa as empathic apprenticeship. *Asia Pacific Viewpoint, 55*(3), 319–330.

Fine, M., & Torre, M. E. (2021). *Essentials of critical participatory action research*. American Psychological Association.

Finlay, L. (2002). Negotiating the swamp: The opportunity and challenge of reflexivity in research practice. *Qualitative Research: QR, 2*(2), 209–230. https://doi.org/10.1177/146879410200200205

Fook, J. (1993). *Radical casework: A theory of practice*. Allen & Unwin.

Fook, J. (2008). Foreword: Critical reflection and the professional task. In R. Pockett & R. Giles (Eds.), *Critical reflection: Generating theory from practice. The graduating social work student experience*. Darlington Press.

Fook, J. (2016). *Social work: A critical approach to practice*. Sage.

Fook, J., & Gardner, F. (2007). *Practising critical reflection: A resource handbook*. Open University Press.

Geia, L. K., Hayes, B., & Usher, K. (2013). Yarning/Aboriginal storytelling: Towards an understanding of an Indigenous perspective and its implications for research practice. *Contemporary Nurse: A Journal for the Australian Nursing Profession, 46*(1), 13–17. https://doi.org/10.5172/conu.2013.46.1.13

Glaser, B. G., & Strauss, A. (1967). *The discovery of grounded theory: Strategies for qualitative research*. Aldine.

Greenwood, D. J., & Levin, M. (2007). *Introduction to action research* (2nd ed.). Sage.

Haug, F. (Ed.). (1987). *Female sexualization: A collective work of memory*. Verso.

Hayes, N. (2000). *Doing psychological research: Gathering and analysing data*. Open University Press.

Herr, K., & Anderson, G. L. (2005). *The action research dissertation: A guide for students and faculty*. Sage Publications, Inc.

Holliday, A. (2007). *Doing and writing qualitative research* (2nd ed.). Sage Publications, Inc.

Ife, J. (2012). *Human rights & social work: Towards rights-based practice* (3rd ed.). Cambridge University Press Textbooks.

Lapadat, J., Black, N., Clark, P., Gremm, R., Lucy, K., Mieke, M., & Quinlan, L. (2010). Life challenge memory work: Using collaborative autobiography to understand ourselves. *The International Journal of Qualitative Methods, 9*, 77–104.

Liamputtong, P. (2020). *Qualitative research methods*. Oxford University Press.

Matua, G. A., & Van Der Wal, D. M. (2015). Differentiating between descriptive and interpretive phenomenological research approaches. *Nurse Researcher, 22*(6), 22. http://dx.doi.org/10.7748/nr.22.6.22.e1344

McCall, S. (2011). *First person plural Aboriginal storytelling and the ethics of collaborative authorship*. UBC Press.

Meo-Sewabu, L. (2014). Cultural discernment as an ethics framework: An indigenous Fijian approach. *Asia Pacific Viewpoint, 55*(3), 345–354. https://doi.org/10.1111/apv.12059

Mezirow, J., & Associates (1991). *Fostering critical reflection in adulthood. A guide to transformative and emancipatory learning*. Jossey-Bass.

Morley, C. (2015). *Practising critical reflection to develop emancipatory change: Challenging the legal response to sexual assault*. Ashgate.

Morley, C., Ablett, P., & Macfarlane, S. (2019). *Engaging with social work*. Cambridge University Press.

Natasi, B. K. (2013). Using multimedia techniques in ethnographic research. In J. J. Schensul & M. D. LeCompte (Eds.), *Specialized ethnographic methods a mixed methods approach* (pp. 301–333). AltaMira Press.

Neubauer, B. E., Witkop, C. T., & Varpio, L. (2019). How phenomenology can help us learn from the experiences of others. *Perspectives on Medical Education, 8*, 90–97. https://doi.org/10.1007/s40037-019-0509-2

Newcomb, M., Saxton, K., Lovrić, E., Harris, S., & Davidson, D. (2023). Creating safety: Group reflections on surviving as a female, social work early career academic in the neoliberal academy. *Qualitative Social Work, 22*(6), 1092–1107.

Onyx, J., & Small, J. (2001). Memory-work: The method. *Qualitative Inquiry, 7*(6), 773–786.

Pease, B. (Ed.). (2020). *Doing critical social work: Transformative practices for social justice.* Routledge.

Rauch, F., Schuster, A., Stern, T., Pribila, M., & Townsend, A. (Eds.). (2014). *Promoting change through action research* (p. 1). SensePublishers.

Ravulo, J. (2016). Pacific epistemologies in professional social work practice, policy and research. *Asia Pacific Journal of Social Work and Development, 26*(4), 191–202. https://doi.org/10.1080/02185385.2016.1234970

Rawsthorne, M., Tseris, E., Howard, A., Terare, M., & Sharma, A. (2024). *Using social research for social justice: An introduction for social work and human services.* Routledge.

Rowe, S., Baldry, E., & Earles, W. (2015). Decolonising social work research: Learning from critical Indigenous approaches. *Australian Social Work, 68*(3), 296–308. https://doi.org/10.1080/0312407X.2015.1024264

Sarantakos, S. (2017). *Social research.* Bloomsbury Publishing.

Saxton, K. (2018). Privileging participation in the Pacific: Researcher reflections. *Aotearoa New Zealand Social Work, 30*(4), 9–12.

Saxton, K. (2021). Recontextualizing social work in a globalized world: Lessons from the pacific. In *Practical and political approaches to recontextualizing social work* (pp. 192–208). IGI Global.

Schön, D. (1983). *The reflective practitioner.* Temple Smith.

Schön, D. (1987). *Educating the reflective practitioner.* Jossey-Bass.

Schratz, M., Walker, R., & Schratz-Hadwich, B. (1995). Collective memory-work: The self as a resource for research. In M. Schratz & R. Walker (Eds.), *Research as social change: New opportunities for qualitative research.* Routledge.

Seremetakis, C. N. (2017). *An introduction to cultural anthropology.* Cambridge Scholars Publishing.

Shaw, I., & Gould, N. (Eds.). (2002). *Qualitative research in social work.* SAGE Publications, Ltd.

Shaw, I., & Holland, S. (2014). *Doing qualitative research in social work.* SAGE Publications, Ltd. https://doi.org/10.4135/9781473906006

Smith, L. T. (2021). *Decolonizing methodologies: Research and indigenous peoples.* Bloomsbury Publishing.

Tamasese, K., Peteru, C., Waldegrave, C., & Busch, A. (2005). Ole Taeao Afua, the new morning: A qualitative investigation into Samoan perspectives on mental health and culturally appropriate services. *Australian and New Zealand Journal of Psychiatry, 39*, 300–309.

Teng, F. (2020). A narrative inquiry of identity construction in academic communities of practice: Voices from a Chinese doctoral student in Hong Kong. *Pedagogies: An International Journal, 15*(1), 40–59. httsp://doi.org/10.1080/1554480X.2019.1673164

Tenny, S., Brannan, G. D., Brannan, J. M., & Sharts-Hopko, N. C. (2022). Qualitative study. *StatPearls [Internet].* https://pubmed.ncbi.nlm.nih.gov/29262162/

Vaka, S., Brannelly, T., & Huntington, A. (2016). Getting to the heart of the story: Using Talanoa to explore Pacific mental health. *Issues in Mental Health Nursing, 37*(8), 537–544.

Walters, M. (1980). Signs of the times: Clifford Geertz and Historians. *Theory and Social History,* 537–556.

Walters, M. (2019). *Social research methods* (4th ed.). Oxford University Press.

Weate, J. (2021). Fanon, Merleau-Ponty, and the difference of phenomenology. In *Fanon, phenomenology, and psychology* (pp. 162–174). Routledge.

Wiles, R., Prosser, J., Bagnoli, A., Clark, A., Davies, K., Holland, S., & Renold, E. (2008). *Visual ethics: Ethical issues in visual research.* Economic and Social Research Council for Research Methods.

Williams, H. (2021). The meaning of "phenomenology": Qualitative and philosophical phenomenological research methods. *The Qualitative Report, 26*(2), 366–385. https://doi.org/10.46743/2160-3715/2021.4587

7 Research Methods in Social Work Research

Chapter Summary

- The chapter introduces five commonly used social research methods – observation and ethnographic work, focus groups, interviews, surveys and content analysis – in addition to arts-based and Indigenous methods.
- Despite research being sometimes viewed as separate from direct practice skills, the skills required for research, such as facilitating focus groups or conducting individual interviews, align with social work practice standards and expectations.
- Indigenous research methods prioritise Indigenous voices and perspectives, challenging colonial-centric paradigms.
- The chapter rejects the idea that social research is inaccessible to social work, emphasising the alignment between social work practice skills, research methods and core values of social justice and respect for persons.

Introduction

The selection of the right research method/s is crucial to being able to answer the research question. In the previous chapter, we presented the analogy of methodology being your 'recipe', or list of ingredients required to undertake your research; methods, thus, are the steps you need to take in order to achieve your research aims. Similar to the methods in a recipe cookbook, methods in social research generally follow a series of steps, or a logical sequence of action from beginning to end. Because of the way in which methods tend to follow a set pattern of steps, it is tempting to jump straight to choosing your methods without taking the time to consider your broader methodology (see Chapter 6). Your methodology and methods need to form a clear alignment and epistemological fit. Just as you can take ingredients in the kitchen – for example, potatoes and orange juice – this does not mean that together, they work well as a combination! By carefully selecting the appropriate ingredients that work well in combination, you will end up with a better outcome. Similarly, your research recipe and chosen method need to be good matches to your conceptual framework. They need to reflect your epistemological position, as well as uphold your ethical stance.

In this chapter, we present five of the most commonly utilised methods in social research – observation and ethnographic work, focus groups, interviews, surveys and content analysis – as well as encouraging researchers to consider creative, arts-based research methods. We also acknowledge the need for First Nations epistemological sovereignty and recognise that First Nations' methods for gathering data, sharing knowledge

DOI: 10.4324/9781003316732-7

and storytelling have existed for millennia. As we have consistently highlighted in this book, research is a political project; a process by which certain knowledges are prioritised and voices are privileged. Social workers need to be aware of the ways in which research can be used to serve, maintain or disrupt the status quo, and that without ethical rigour and commitment to reflexivity, social research can be used to maintain colonial forces and empirical paradigms which only further marginalised the populations social workers along which social workers are positioned to work (Tascon & Ife, 2020). This chapter concludes by identifying a range of social work practice skills that are required to successfully undertake research methods and places emphasis on the way in which key social work skills are highly applicable and transferable to research contexts.

Observation and Ethnographic Methods

In Chapter 6, we provided an overview of ethnography as a research methodology in which the researcher becomes immersed in the research environment. Sometimes, the researcher is an outsider entering the research landscape, or, ideally, the researcher is part of the community (e.g. First Nations, LGBTQIA+, sex workers) and engages in a process of researching 'with' participants rather than researching 'on'. There are a range of ethnographic methods from which a researcher may draw, including visual mediums such as photography and film (Glaw et al., 2017), as well as written mediums based on observation, field or memory work. Approaches like critical reflection and participatory action research (PAR) have also been talked about in Chapter 6 as ethnographic tools. There is debate as to whether PAR and critical reflection can rightly be considered methods or methodologies, as Reason and Bradbury (2006) argue that participatory action research is more of an approach to inquiry than a methodology per se. In this book, both have been included in the methodology chapter under the reasoning that they are informed by a particular set of epistemological understandings and axiology and that the process of undertaking critical reflection or action research is further determined by methods such as individual interviews, focus groups, shared reflection/memory making, deconstruction-reconstruction, journaling and so forth. Ultimately, the debate as to whether these should be rightly considered methods or methodologies, particularly within a post-modern context, can never be truly answered. As such, we feel that it is more important for emerging researchers to recognise that their choice of methodology and methods is aligned to a certain epistemological and ideological basis. In choosing what methodology or method to use in conducting social research, we should be cognisant of our ethical mandate to pursue a research agenda aligned with social work values of social justice, human rights and self-determination.

Observations are particularly valuable in gaining firsthand insights into human behaviour, distinct from self-reported behaviours or opinions (Busetto et al., 2020). Broadly, observations can be divided into the categories of insider–outsider research (Braun & Clarke, 2013). In insider observations, the observer is an active participant of the research context and is considered integrated into the society or group (Bukamal, 2022) An example of this might be a youth worker observing experiences within a youth detention centre. Conversely, outsider observations occur when the researcher deliberately seeks to maintain a distance from the context or scenario in the hope of minimising interference (Holmes, 2020). This style of observation is more common in psychology or biomedical research: for example, the psychologist may observe the way young people interact with staff when detained in a youth detention facility. In social research, positionality is of utmost importance, including a recognition of how your own position influences the world around you and the way in which you view and observe the world (Bryman, 2016). The insider–outsider research binary is limited in the sense that it may not recognise that people can be both insiders and outsiders of multiple communities and have intersecting identities (Holmes, 2020). However, it does help us to understand the differences between ethnographic methodologies that research on rather than with participants. If deciding to engage in systematic observations of a group or community of which you are not a part, ethical questions as to the privacy and data sovereignty of such processes need to be unpacked. For more on this, see Chapter 3.

The documentation of observations can occur in a number of ways. This could be through field notes, journals, record keeping, incident reports, voice memos or drawing of pictures and images (or a combination). Throughout the observation process, the observer meticulously records notes encompassing the entirety of observed occurrences or, alternatively, focusing on predetermined elements, such as interactions between staff and young people or communication among distinct subgroups such as youth workers and 'detainees'. The documentation of these notes may occur contemporaneously or post-observation, often depending on how practical it is to take notes at the time of the event/observation as well as ethical considerations. Examples of field notes are the researcher's notes taken at regular intervals (for example, morning tea, lunch, afternoon tea) or writing down the details of the conversation as soon as practical following the event (Dunk-West, 2018). The use of photographic journaling and video blogging, including online blogging mediums, is also gaining popularity as a tool in ethnographic research. But the use of publicly accessible internet forums and online technology may raise its own set of ethical considerations that need to be thought through.

Focus Groups

Focus groups, sometimes referred to as group interviews, are often used in qualitative research as a data collection method. Focus groups can be structured, semi-structured or unstructured. While unstructured individual interviews require a lot of planning from the interviewer, unstructured focus groups can rely more on the interactive dynamic of the group (Morgan, 2019). Participants in focus groups may have a shared experience or interest in the research topic (Ravitch & Carl, 2016; Travers, 2019); however, participants also have their own diverse backgrounds, experiences, worldviews and interpretations of the research topic. This diversity can allow for a wide range of data to be collected and act as a way to prompt participants to reflect on or share their experiences from a perspective they may not have been considered in an individual interview.

Focus groups are also a helpful way of generating a lot of data at once because they create interactive discussions amongst the participants (Walter, 2019). Although focus groups are often considered to be an efficient and inexpensive data collection method, the purpose of a focus group is not to simply complete as many interviews as possible at once. Rather, it is to develop an interactive discussion between participants, a process Morgan (2019) describes as "sharing and comparing". Through sharing, participants can discover their similarities. An example of this is when one participant shares an experience, such as "When I first noticed my hearing loss, I felt embarrassed and didn't want to go out any more" and then another participant recognises the similarities in their own experience and builds on and responds to the first person's experience, such as, "I felt the same way. I stopped going to family events because I was embarrassed at how many times I had to ask someone to repeat themselves". Conversely, through comparing, participants can examine their differences by speaking of how their experience or understanding of a situation was different. An example of this may look like, "I didn't feel that way. I found my family and friends were very accommodating to me and always made sure to speak loudly and clearly". In this way, focus groups enable an organic narrative to emerge and centralise the participants' own voices within the research.

In many First Nations and Pacific Island epistemologies, this process of shared dialogue or discussion is the process by which events and phenomena are given shared meaning (Vaka et al., 2016). The existence of both informal and formal processes for facilitation dialogue (e.g. yarning, talanoa, talking circles) that exist throughout Indigenous cultural groups highlights the way in which 'focus groups' is not a concept unique to Western research contexts, although quite often, Western research institutions have rejected Indigenous knowledge basis as lacking research awareness and epistemological rigour (Smith, 2021). Added to this, research methods that prioritise participant voices and value lived experiences have a strong alignment to feminist, narrative, decolonising and anti-oppressive practice frameworks. It is important that the voices and research contribution of focus group participants are further valued during the analysis phase, whereby the researcher must be cognisant of their own positionality and lens by which they are interpreting results. This is explored further in Chapters 8 and 9.

Although most researchers will discuss issues of privacy and confidentiality prior to commencing the focus group, there are very real challenges with regards to confidentiality because the researcher cannot control the actions of other participants in the group or what information group participants may or may not divulge to others. Focus groups can also run the risk of one person taking over or dominating the conversation, which can lead to problems of conformity, where the rest of the participants go along with the dominant voice (Meško, 2022). On the other hand, focus groups may bolster the confidence of other group members to articulate their views, knowing that their experiences and beliefs are shared by others (Stewart & Shamdasani, 2014). In certain cultural contexts in which knowledge generation is seen as a collective process and in which no single voice should be prioritised over the collective good, the potential downsides of focus groups may be outweighed by the cultural and epistemological alignment of focus group approaches.

Interviews

Interviewing is a key skill widely used by social workers in order to learn more information about an individual, community or group. In a similar vein, interviews are a popular research method utilised by social work researchers due to the way in which interviews can harbour in-depth information (Dunk-West, 2018). Using interviews as the data collection method in a research design involves the researcher engaging in a one-on-one conversation with a participant to gather in-depth and detailed information about their perspectives, opinions and experiences about the research topic (Tracy, 2013). Given the one-to-one nature of interviews, it is important to consider the power dynamics in the interviewer–interviewee relationship: Are both people of the same gender? Are there different cultural considerations? Is English the preferred language of the interviewee, and/or will there be the use of an interpreter? Is there the potential for a power differential due to age differences? Are there connotations linked to people in positions of power and authority and expectations to conform? Are group rather than individual conversations more congruent with cultural beliefs and practices that value collectivism? These are just some examples of ethical and practical questions that need to be asked when deciding whether to utilise interviews in your research design.

Interviews in research are usually semi-structured or unstructured. Semi-structured interviews involve the researcher asking a series of prepared, open-ended questions. These same questions are usually used in every interview and often asked in the same order. Unstructured interviews are guided by general themes and are more conversation-like. This style is much more flexible and allows the researcher to ask additional questions and further explore issues as the participant raises them (Travers, 2019). While individual interviews are more conversational than structured interviews, there is a significant amount of skill required to ensure important information is not missed or misunderstood and to pick up on emotional cues (Tracy, 2013). Interviews can also be held face-to-face, over the phone or online. Because interviews involve in-depth conversations, it is best to have the interview recorded either through audio or video means so that the data can later be analysed (Travers, 2019). It is important to always advise the participant that it will be recorded and to discuss all relevant privacy and confidentiality issues prior to commencing the interview. As with all research methods utilised in data collection, universities or professional bodies will generally require information about how this recorded data will be stored and managed as well as how participants will be advised of their rights with regards to confidentiality. Because individual interviews are directly between the researcher and the participant, some people may prefer individual interviews rather than group settings so as to protect their anonymity. This may be particularly relevant if the research involves an area of high social stigma, for example, sexually transmitted diseases.

Surveys and Questionnaires

Surveys and questionnaires may be one of the most widely used and popular data collection methods because of their ease of distribution and cost efficiency. They also lend themselves to both qualitative and quantitative methodologies depending on whether the answers are obtained using numerical means or narrative responses. Generally, in qualitative research, the questions asked in a questionnaire will be open-ended, that is, they invite the participant to respond in their own words about a certain topic or experience (Alston & Bowles, 2020). For example, when conducting research into people's attitudes towards youth crime, you may ask an open-ended question such as "What do you think about youth crime?" The benefit of asking such a broad question is that you open yourself to a wide range of data possibilities and responses. However, this also comes with its own risks, as those completing the survey may find your question ambiguous or may interpret the question in a different light to what you intended. So you may decide to refine your questions to be more specific to your topic and research aims: for example, "What do you believe drives rates of youth crime?" or "How should society respond to growing rates of youth crime?" The process of developing a methodologically robust questionnaire or survey is time-consuming and requires careful consideration and refinement (Walter, 2019). Researchers should not be tempted to choose this method solely on the basis of time constraints or to expedite the research process. Good research takes time irrespective of the chosen method and tools of data collection.

The terms 'questionnaires' and 'surveys' are often used interchangeably. However, a questionnaire tends to focus on gathering the views and responses from a particular set or group of people. For example, you may ask young people to complete a questionnaire about their time in a youth detention facility. A survey, arguably, seeks to gather a bigger-picture analysis of the phenomenon under investigation. Especially when combined with demographic data collection, a survey can be used to compare responses between participants as well as to sort by predetermined factors such as age, race, locality, gender or other characteristics. Both surveys and questionnaires may also use what is known as a Likert scale; this is when qualitative responses are assigned a numerical value. For example, I might ask participants to rate their views of social workers on a scale of 1 to 5, with 1 being extremely negative and 5 being positive.

1_____2_____3_____4_____5
Extremely negative   Negative   Neither positive nor negative   Positive
Extremely Positive

Sometimes, Likert scales are also used to replicate studies used in one setting or time period in order to compare and contrast results (Alston & Bowles, 2020). It is more than likely you have come across a Likert scale in your daily life, whether it be to rate your satisfaction as a customer following a phone call to your local utility provider or asked to press a button to signify how happy you are with the cleanliness level of the bathrooms at the airport. There widespread use attests to their functionality and variability as a data collection method. There is also a range of both free and paid software that can assist researchers in gathering survey and questionnaire data (for example, SurveyMonkey, Qualtrix). As with any data collection tool, data gathering should not be assumed as objective and apolitical, and a thorough consideration of ethical impacts needs to be worked through during the research design stage.

Content Analysis

Content analysis is the analysis of some form of communication for patterns or trends. This communication can be in written, audio or visual forms and is drawn from preexisting (sometimes known as secondary) data. Secondary data is data that has already been collected for some other analytic purpose (for example, patient records, census data, governmental reports). While content analysis may draw from secondary data sources, it can also use sources of communication (not limited to) policy documents, online content such as Facebook posts, advertising materials, graffiti, cartoons, portraits, photographs of a particular area/topic/subject/experience, films, music and a range of other audio-visual means. What is important to acknowledge when conducting content analysis is not just what is written/documented but also what *isn't* being said (Alston & Bowles, 2020). For example, when reviewing newspaper articles about youth crime, do the stories all tend to represent young people from a particular race? Do the views of business owners feature more (or less) than the views of caregivers? Do they focus more in regional or urban communities? Understanding what is being written and depicted and interpreting what is being said is often just as important as understanding what isn't being said.

Naming content analysis as a method may seem confusing because of the fact that it has the word 'analysis' in the title. However, what this is referring to is the process of gathering some sort of pre-existing data or 'content' that will then be analysed. *How* the researcher decides to then analyse this information then depends on the theoretical lens and analytical framework they have chosen to employ (see Chapters 2 and 8). For example, you may choose to understand attitudes towards youth crime but gather recent and/or historical newspaper articles that feature stories about youth offending. The 'content' in this instance is the newspaper articles. However, how you choose to analyse, interpret and understand these articles will be dependent on your epistemological position and theoretical viewpoint, also known as your analytical framework" or instead of aka. For example, you may choose to apply a feminist, narrative or discourse analysis, or you may decide to look at where in the newspaper the articles were placed or what newspaper source featured the most articles. The *what* of your research is determined by the type of content; *how* you understand this content is determined by your analytical framework. As such, you can see how research design is an intricate web of epistemology, axiology, methodology, methods and analysis, all playing an important role in the construction of how you understand and attempt to answer questions about self and society.

Indigenous Methods

Indigenous research methods challenge a historically colonial-centric and frequently exploitative research paradigm, aiming instead to prioritise the voices and perspectives of Indigenous peoples within the framework of social justice (McEntyre et al., 2019). In recent years, the importance of Indigenous lead and informed research has gained growing acceptance as the best-practice approach to engaging with issues that impact First Nations communities (Drawson et al., 2017). Despite this growing recognition, Indigenous populations globally continue to face systemic barriers in terms of racism, access to education, economic resources, social inclusion, political representation and the impacts of climate change (Sherwood, 2010). Because of the inequity of health and well-being outcomes for First Nations communities (particularly within white settler colonies) and ongoing disadvantage, First Nations communities are thus thrust into the research spotlight and become the focus of many social research projects as well as policy decisions more often than not led by the white so called expert (Chilisa, 2019; Wilson, 2008). In such instances, First Nations communities are often problematised, and the focus is on health and well-being disparities and is conducted using processes designed and developed by white policymakers and academics (Bishen & Pellissery, 2023; Alatas, 2022). Wade Nobles (1976) coined the term 'scientific colonialism' to describe this process whereby the impact of colonisation drives social inequality, and then this social inequality is used to justify actions driven and informed by the white Western majority to further justify policy and decision-making regarding First Nations communities. As such, there is a phenomenon of First Nations peoples being over researched on and yet under-represented in the design and benefits of the research process (Chilisa, 2019; Alatas, 2022).

Not surprisingly, Indigenous writers, leaders and academics have been calling for some time for epistemological sovereignty in the design and delivery of research processes that directly impact their communities (Dew et al., 2019; Smith, 2021). Although the social sciences have acknowledged the importance of valuing First Nations ways of being, knowing and doing, the process by which social research is validated through Western institutions and processes (see Chapters 2 and 10) means that Indigenous knowledges are still expected to operate within a Western research world in order to be legitimised and validated (Smith, 2021; Hayward et al., 2021; McGuire-Adams, 2020; Bennett, 2021). Truly decolonising and Indigenous-centred research rejects Western epistemological privileging (Hayward et al., 2021) and demands that Indigenous research should not be required to meet Western academic and 'scientific' standards in order to be published or viewed as statistically significant (Bennett, 2020). As Baskin (2005, p. 174) posits, "an agenda for

Aboriginal research must focus on the goals and processes of decolonisation and self-determination. A research project that does not contribute in some way to these objects is not worth doing".

In Australia, any research involving Aboriginal and/or Torres Strait Islanders is expected to meet the *Ethical conduct in research with Aboriginal and Torres Strait Islander Peoples and communities: Guidelines for researchers and stakeholders*, developed by the National Health and Medical Health Research Council and to engage with The *AIATSIS Code of Ethics for Aboriginal and Torres Strait Islander Research* (The AIATSIS Code, 2020). These documents are designed to ensure that research with and about Aboriginal and Torres Strait Islander peoples follows a process of meaningful engagement and reciprocity between the researcher and the individuals and/or communities involved in the research (NHMRC, 2018; AIATSIS, 2020). Similar guidelines exist in Canada, New Zealand and the United States. These guidelines act as a tool to help ensure cultural safety is prioritised and cultural protocols are observed and are a minimum requirement for any researcher planning to conduct research involving Aboriginal communities (Humphery, 2003). However, these guidelines do not explicitly name methodological requirements and are often used by non-Indigenous researchers conducting work within First Nations communities in order to validate their own research agendas. That is not to say that non-Indigenous researchers should be excluded from participating in research involving First Nations communities (although there are arguments in support of this, too) but rather to highlight that NHMRC research guidelines are aimed at doing the least amount of harm within communities rather than challenging Western hegemonic dominance within research processes. As articulated by Rigney (1999), Indigenous research methodology has at its core the principals of resistance as an emancipatory imperative, political integrity and the privileging of Indigenous voices in Indigenous research. One of the best ways to privilege Indigenous voices is to utilise First Nations methods and to prioritise Indigenous worldviews rather than requiring research to be validated by a predetermined Western framework of what constitutes legitimate knowledge (Bennett, 2020; Smith, 2021). For this reason, First Nations or Indigenous research that is written by members and representatives of the Indigenous community for the sole benefit of the community members would best align with a decolonising and social justice research prerogative.

Arts-Based Methods

Arts-based methods are a rapidly growing research genre that seeks to make social research engaging and more publicly accessible (Gioia & Leavy, 2020). It involves the use of creative mediums to address social research questions in an iterative way in which theory and practice are intertwined. The forms in which research 'data' can be collected and expressed are many, including (but not limited to) novels, novellas, poetry, short stories, dance, drama, graphic novels, painting, sculpture, graffiti, collages, quilts, puppetry, needlework, baking, films, song, musical scores, rap and photography (Leavy, 2022). Arts-based research methods, sometimes also referred to as creative inquiry or arts-based inquiry, recognise the barriers to research translation within academic contexts; namely, that research articles are written by academics for other academics. In response, arts-based research places the inquiry process at the centre, that is, the process of meaning making is just as important as the 'outcome' itself. In arts-based research, the participant is an active and creative agent in the process of meaning making rather than a passive recipient being researched on. This makes arts-based research well suited to the participatory and democratic aims of social work. Arts-based methods in qualitative research are highly applicable where research aims are to explore, understand, uncover or disrupt (Leavy, 2020).

Arts-based methods have gained recognition as an effective and acceptable method for qualitative research and are becoming more widely used in multiple disciplines (Pain, 2012). Arts-based methods can be undertaken as an auto-ethnographic endeavour, or they can occur in a collective or community-based setting. Part of the appeal is the way in which community members and research constituents can become involved in the research process through the creation of art in its various 'shapes' and forms (Leavy, 2020). Arts-based research seeks to bridge the divide between researcher and the public by using creative mediums that speak across educational and language divides. For this reason, arts-based research may be seen as congruent with the emancipatory aims of social work and other 'helping' professions (Richards & Roth, 2019). Although there may be different terms used to describe arts-based research, this should not be confused as one approach being better or more 'right' than another. Such debates detract from the purpose of arts-based research, which is to ensure research processes are accessible and multiple forms of knowledge and knowledge transference are valued (Archibald & Blines, 2021). It is precisely its transformational capacity that makes arts-based research both threatening to the academy and a source of empowerment for many otherwise marginalised and silenced groups in society.

Applying Social Work Skills

In 2023, the Australian Association of Social Workers (AASW) released an updated set of practice standards. These standards outline the expectations for social work graduates across a number of diverse knowledge and skill sets and assert a position that is "open to new and emerging knowledge, research and evidence informing" (AASW, 2023, p. 15). Despite this, research is often viewed as being superfluous to social work practice, particularly by social work students who have a focus on obtaining skills to be 'work ready' (Macken et al., 2021; Morley et al., 2017). Contrary to the belief that research is somehow separate to direct practice skills, the skills required to engage in high-quality, meaningful and ethical research have direct transferability to diverse fields of social work practice. Take, for example, the skills required for facilitating a focus group; not only does this draw on facilitation skills, but there is also a need to understand theories of group work and group processes as well as the ability to manage power dynamics and establish a culturally safe environment in which to hold conversations (Alston & Bowles, 2020; Walter, 2019). Notwithstanding the points we make about the Australian context, internationally, at the very least, social work students graduate into a world in which they will need to update their knowledge, and research literacy is crucial to this end.

Conversely, when conducting individual interviews, the researcher needs to be able to communicate ideas effectively, attentively listen and demonstrate a high level of interpersonal communication skills, respond to verbal and non-verbal cues and check with participants to clarify meaning (Walter, 2019). These interview techniques are used in a number of settings in which social workers are required to conduct 'assessments', 'needs analysis' or, in more decolonising language, effectively engage with individuals, groups and families. In fact, at every stage of the research process, there is a range of skills required that have a clear synergy with the practice standards and professional expectations of social work and other helping professions. This includes the ability to work with persons of diverse backgrounds, genders and abilities and ensure a high level of ethical rigour and professional accountability. The table that follows outlines some further examples of research methods and their alignment with social work practice skills.

Applying Social Work Practice Skills in Research

Research Method	Examples of Social Work Practice Skills Required
Ethnography	Observation, journalling, note taking, critical reflection, cultural responsivity
Interviews	Rapport building, paraphrasing, questioning, active listening, summarising
Focus Groups	Group facilitation, negotiation, relationship building, interpersonal communication, self-awareness, empathy
Content Analysis	Data management, ethical decision-making, critical thinking, application of theory to practise
Surveys/Questionnaires	Planning, organisation, high-level written communication, prioritising

Choosing the Right Method

The selection of which method to use depends on both the theoretical framework of the researcher as well as which method will likely support the aims of the research. Your choice of method also needs to uphold an ethical framework conducive to both the theoretical and ideological positioning of social work. For example, as a researcher, I may be drawn to ethnography because of its strong history in researching cultural experiences and thus decide I want to use this methodology to research suicidality among young Aboriginal men living in rural communities. I may decide that I want to undertake observation, primarily by using photographs to capture images that represent grief and loss. Although on paper, this approach would be a practical method, from an ideological and epistemological position, this approach is problematic. First, unless I identify as being from this community, the insider/outsider positionality and phenomenon of subjugating Indigenous communities as a passive object to be researched 'on' reinforces colonial practices and does little to provide opportunities for alternative voices in research (Bennett, 2020; Smith, 2021). This is particularly if the analysis and interpretation of the observations is done from a lens counter to the cultural context in which lived experiences are best understood (Chilisa, 2019; Rigney, 1999). Second, for some communities, the use of photographs is not culturally appropriate, and this may be particularly so if these images depict persons that are now deceased (Vicente & Azoulay, 2020). Similarly, the use of photographs that depict artefacts or symbols of cultural significance, particularly without permission, is a form of theft, violating the rights of one group for the sake of the researcher's own curiosity or 'interest' (Tynan, 2023). Ultimately, any research involving First Nations communities is done on the invitation of community and led by community (Bennett, 2020), in which case ethnographic methods may apply. Conversely, for the same research project, the researcher may decide to facilitate individual interviews by which participants can select what information participants choose to share, when and how. This example may seem trite, and it is not the intention of this chapter to oversimplify the ongoing impact of colonisation and the need to recognise Indigenous epistemological sovereignty in research but rather to re-emphasise the importance of methodological rigour in social research and, in particular, an approach to research design that aligns with the methodological objectives of the project but simultaneously upholds the social justice mandate of critical social work.

This chapter also calls for ongoing recognition of research processes that centre First Nations epistemologies and research methods. In emphasising the importance of First Nations–led and informed research, we want to avoid any process whereby First Nations methods or knowledge basis are commodified for personal gain or crudely summarised in ways which may facilitate further cultural appropriation of First Nations practices. In highlighting the significance of Indigenous research in social research, we recognise what Bindi Bennett (2020) outlines as the phenomenon whereby non-Indigenous researchers often seek to benefit from utilising Indigenous methods and research approaches. Such research instances, despite the researcher being 'well meaning' or a self-identified 'ally', further risk the dispossession of Indigenous knowledges and bolster colonial forces within research, social and academic institutions. While celebrating Indigenous practices and calling out Eurocentrism within dominant social research discourse, we recognise that the commodification of Indigenous methods is deeply problematic, particularly when knowledge is not 'owned' by any one individual and that (white) social researchers have, unfortunately, a long history of benefiting from research on Indigenous communities (Hayward et al., 2021; Saxton, 2018; Sherwood, 2010). In line with principles of social justice, and recognising First Nations sovereignty, we recognise the limitations of our Western knowledge basis and bias in writing this chapter. We similarly request all social workers to be aware of their own positionality, motivations and the overt way in which research has and continues to be used to perpetuate oppression, colonisation and epistemicide.

Conclusion

The selection of your research method is pivotal in both achieving your research aims and ensuring social research maintains a commitment to social justice and ethical integrity. Aligning methodology and methods, particularly in social work, requires careful consideration of epistemological fit and ethical principles. In this chapter, we explored five widely used methods in social research – observation and ethnography, focus groups, interviews, surveys and content analysis. We hope that this chapter can provide the reader with a basic awareness of different research methods and facilitate a desire to learn further about the ways in which certain research methods may best be an appropriate fit for your chosen area of research or proposed study. Additionally, we advocate for the consideration of creative, arts-based research methods and acknowledge a long established tradition of research and knowledge transmission used by First Nations communities. Although this chapter underscores the ongoing importance of recognising and centering First Nations epistemologies and research methods, we caution against their commodification for personal gain and have sought to avoid a summarisation of Indigenous methods that may inadvertently contribute to cultural appropriation. We hear the voices of our Indigenous colleagues who have emphasised the risk of non-Indigenous researchers benefiting from Indigenous methods (even with good intentions), which can perpetuate dispossession of Indigenous knowledge and reinforce colonial forces within research and academic institutions. Last, we reject the premise that social research is inaccessible or irrelevant to social work and draw clear synergies between social work practice skills and research methods and alignment with the core values of social justice and respect for persons. By re-emphasising the inherently political nature of research, we stress the imperative for social researchers to be aware of, name and engage with their own worldviews when considering the best method to support their research aims and the social justice prerogative of social work.

Further Reading

Alatas, S. F. (2016). Captive mind. In G. Ritzer (Ed.), *The Blackwell encyclopedia of sociology*. John Wiley & Sons, Ltd. https://doi.org/10.1002/9781405165518.wbeosc006.pub2

Bennett, B. (2020). Chapter 3 Acknowledgements in aboriginal social work research: How to counteract neo-colonial academic complacency. In S. Tascon & J. Ife (Eds.), *Disrupting whiteness in social work* (1st ed., pp. 91–107). Routledge. https://doi.org/10.4324/9780429284182-7

Braun, V., & Clarke, V. (2013). *Successful qualitative research: A practical guide for beginners*. Sage.

Chilisa, B. (2019). *Indigenous research methodologies*. SAGE Publications.

Leavy, P. (2022). *Research design: Quantitative, qualitative, mixed methods, arts-based, and community-based participatory research approaches*. Guilford Publications.

Saxton, K. (2018). Privileging participation in the Pacific: Researcher reflections. *Aotearoa New Zealand Social Work*, 30(4), 9–12.

Smith, L. T. (2021). *Decolonizing methodologies: Research and indigenous peoples* (3rd ed.). Bloomsbury.

References

AASW. (2023). *AASW practice standards*. Australian Association of Social Workers. https://aasw-prod.s3.ap-southeast-2.amazonaws.com/wp-content/uploads/2023/05/AASW-Practice-Standards-FEB2023–1.pdf

Alatas, S. F. (2022). Alatas on colonial and autonomous knowledge. *Syed Hussein Alatas and Critical Social Theory: Decolonizing the Captive Mind*, 233.

Alston, M., & Bowles, W. (2020). *Research for social workers: An Introduction to methods* (4th ed.). Routledge.

Archibald, M., & Blines, J. (2021). Metaphors in the making: Illuminating the process of arts-based health research through a case exemplar linking arts-based, qualitative and quantitative research data. *International Journal of Qualitative Methods*, 20. https://doi.org/10.1177/1609406920987954

Australian Institute of Aboriginal and Torres Strait Islander Studies. (2020). *AIATSIS code of ethics for Aboriginal and Torres Strait Islander research*. AIATSIS. https://aiatsis.gov.au/sites/default/files/2022-02/aiatsis-code-ethics-jan22.pdf

Baskin, C. (2005). Storytelling circles: Reflections on Aboriginal protocols in research. *Canadian Social Work Review*, 22(2), 171–187.

Bennett, B. (2020). Chapter 3 Acknowledgements in Aboriginal social work research: How to counteract neo-colonial academic complacency. In S. Tascon & J. Ife (Eds.), *Disrupting whiteness in social work* (1st ed., pp. 91–107). Routledge. https://doi.org/10.4324/9780429284182-7

Bennett, B. (2021). *Aboriginal fields of practice*. Bloomsbury Publishing.

Bishen, A., & Pellissery, S. (2023). 'It is identity, stupid': How captive minds work in contexts of decision making, June 1, 2023. https://ssrn.com/abstract=4507008 or http://dx.doi.org/10.2139/ssrn.4507008

Bryman, A. (2016). *Social research methods* (5th ed.). Oxford University Press.

Bukamal, H. (2022). Deconstructing insider – outsider researcher positionality. *British Journal of Special Education*, 49(3), 327–349.

Busetto, L., Wick, W., & Gumbinger, C. (2020). How to use and assess qualitative research methods. *Neurological Research and Practice*, 2, 14. https://doi.org/10.1186/s42466-020-00059-z

Chilisa, B. (2019). *Indigenous research methodologies*. SAGE Publications.

Dew, A., McEntyre, E., & Vaughan, P. (2019). Taking the research journey together: The insider and outsider experiences of Aboriginal and non-Aboriginal researchers. *Forum Qualitative Sozialforschung Forum: Qualitative Social Research*, 20(1). https://doi.org/10.17169/fqs-20.1.3156

Drawson, A. S., Toombs, E., & Mushquash, C. (2017). Indigenous research methods: A systematic review. *The International Indigenous Policy Journal, 8*(2).

Dunk-West, P. (2018). *How to be a social worker: A critical guide for students* (2nd ed.). Palgrave Macmillan.

Gioia, C., & Leavy, P. (2020). Arts-based research: Merging social research and the creative arts. In L. Patricia (Ed.), *The Oxford handbook of qualitative research* (2nd ed.). Oxford Handbooks (2020; online edn, Oxford Academic, 2 Sept. 2020). https://doi.org/10.1093/oxfordhb/9780190847388.013.27, accessed 29 October, 2023.

Glaw, X., Inder, K., Kable, A., & Hazelton, M. (2017). Visual methodologies in qualitative research: Autophotography and photo elicitation applied to mental health research. *International Journal of Qualitative Methods, 16*(1), 1609406917748215.

Hayward, A., Wodtke, L., Craft, A., Robin, T., et al. (2021). Addressing the need for indigenous and decolonized quantitative research methods in Canada. *SSM – Population Health, 15*.

Holmes, A. G. D. (2020). Researcher positionality – a consideration of its influence and place in qualitative research – a new researcher guide. *Shanlax International Journal of Education, 8*(4), 1–10.

Humphery, K. (2003). Setting the rules: The development of the NHMRC guidelines on ethical matters in Aboriginal and Torres Strait Islander health research. *New Zealand Bioethics Journal, 4*(1), 14–19.

Leavy, P. (2020). *Method meets art: Arts-based research practice.* Guilford Publications.

Macken, C., Hare, J., Souter, K., Macken, C., Hare, J., & Souter, K. (2021). Learning and teaching in higher education. *Seven Radical Ideas for the Future of Higher Education: An Australian Perspective*, 33–52.

McEntyre, E., Vaughan, P., & Dew, A. (2019). Taking the research journey together: The insider and outsider experiences of Aboriginal and non-Aboriginal researchers. *Forum Qualitative Sozialforschung/Forum: Qualitative Social Research, 20*(1), 1–17. https://doi.org/10.17169/fqs-20.1.3156

McGuire-Adams, T. D. (2020). Paradigm shifting: Centering Indigenous research methodologies, an Anishinaabe perspective. *Qualitative Research in Sport, Exercise and Health, 12*(1), 34–47. https://doi.org/10.1080/2159676X.2019.1662474

Mesko, G. & Hacin, R. (2022). Focus Groups: The challenges and advantages of creating and using focus groups in rural areas? In *Research Methods for Rural Criminologists* (p. 115–126) editors Weisheit, R.A, Peterson, J. & Pytlarz, A. Routledge.

Morgan, D. (2019). *Basic and advanced focus groups.* SAGE Publications, Inc. https://doi.org/10.4135/9781071814307

Morley, C., MacFarlane, S., & Ablett, P. (2017). The neoliberal colonisation of social work education: A critical analysis and practices for resistance. *Advances in Social Work and Welfare Education, 19*(2), 25–40.

NHMRC. (2018). *Ethical conduct in research with Aboriginal and Torres Strait Islander peoples and communities: Guidelines for researchers and stakeholders.* National Health and Medical Research Council, Commonwealth of Australia.

Nobles, W. W. (1976). Extended self: Rethinking the so-called Negro self-concept. *Journal of Black Psychology, 2*(2), 15–24.

Pain, H. (2012). A literature review to evaluate the choice and use of visual methods. *International Journal of Qualitative Methods, 11*, 303–319.

Ravitch, S. M., & Carl, N. M. (2016). *Qualitative research: Bridging the conceptual, theoretical and methodological.* Sage Publication.

Reason, P., & Bradbury, H. (Eds.). (2006). *Handbook of action research.* Sage.

Richards, J. C., & Roth, W. M. (2019). *Empowering students as self-directed learners of qualitative research methods: Transformational practices for instructors and students* (Vol. 6). Brill.

Rigney, L. I. (1999). Internationalization of an indigenous anticolonial cultural critique of research methodologies: A guide to indigenist research methodology and its principles. *Journal for Native American Studies, Wicazo Sa Review, 14*(2), 109–113.

Sherwood, J. (2010). *Do no harm: Decolonising Aboriginal health research*, PhD thesis. Faculty of Arts and Social Sciences, University of New South Wales, Australia. https://unsworks.unsw.edu.au/bitstreams/3835b8d9-f63f-4dc4-91b1-d31525a4c32d/download

Smith, L. T. (2021). *Decolonizing methodologies: Research and indigenous peoples*. Bloomsbury Publishing.

Stewart, D. W., & Shamdasani, P. N. (2014). *Focus groups: Theory and practice* (Vol. 20). Sage Publications.

Tracy, S. J. (2013). *Qualitative research methods: Collecting evidence, crafting analysis, communicating impact*. John Wiley & Sons, Incorporated.

Travers, M. (2019). Qualitative interviewing methods. In M. Walter (Ed.), *Social research methods* (4th ed., ebook). Oxford University Press.

Tynan, L. (2023). Data collection versus knowledge theft: Relational accountability and the research ethics of indigenous knowledges. In *Challenging global development: Towards decoloniality and justice* (pp. 139–164). Springer Nature.

Vaka, S., Brannelly, T., & Huntington, A. (2016). Getting to the heart of the story: Using Talanoa to explore Pacific mental health. *Issues in Mental Health Nursing*, 37(8), 537–544.

Vicente, F. L., & Azoulay, A. A. (2020). In their own words. *Análise Social*, 55(235), 417–436.

Walter, M. (2019). *Social research methods* (4th ed.). Oxford University Press.

Wilson, S. (2008). *Research is ceremony: Indigenous research methods*. Fernwood Publishing.

8   Data Analysis

Chapter Summary

- The process of data analysis involves examining words, language, symbols and their respective meanings. When engaging in data analysis, you employ your analytical perspective to interpret the words conveyed by research participants.
- The coding of qualitative data is an iterative process informed by the specific objectives of your research and in line with your epistemological views.
- Data analysis can be deductive, that is, data is coded according to existing theory and/or research structures, or inductive, where theory is generated as a result of coding.
- At this stage of history, computer software and artificial intelligence cannot do the research for us, but they can greatly assist in managing the data and assisting us to categorise it into themes.

In this chapter, the means through which data are analysed are examined, including the use of qualitative software to capture themes and code data. The reader is taken through the process of 'coding' and invited to reflect on inductive and deductive approaches to data collection and analysis as they relate to their chosen methodology (see Chapter 6) and research goals. Although this chapter is largely procedurally driven in that it describes how to code data, it will examine different types of data and connect this to the previous chapter about research methods. Types of data are presented, as well as different ways to code and categorise data to ultimately inform your data analysis. The chapter will take the same approach to coding that we saw in Chapter 3: just as research questions require narrowing down, so too does the process of coding require a clearly defined 'narrowing down' process. We will also reiterate the importance of knowing and engaging with your researcher positioning, as your data analysis is inherently linked to your methodology as well as your worldview, or analytical lens (see Chapter 2). A list of further reading is also provided, as this chapter is an overview, not a definitive summation, of data coding and analysis in social research. Your ultimate analytical technique and framework will depend on your research design, epistemological positioning and research goals.

Getting Started With Analysis

Qualitative data analysis doesn't have to be overwhelming; essentially, you are grouping your data or 'findings' into key themes or categories. Having said that, it is important not to underestimate the amount of time needed for the coding and analysis stage of your research (Anastas & MacDonald, 2000). Whether your approach to data analysis is

DOI: 10.4324/9781003316732-8

deductive (top down) or inductive (bottom up) will determine how you commence your analytical journey. This is informed by your methodology and how you view knowledge generation and construction. At this point of the research journey, your research project is like a jigsaw puzzle, with the different pieces (e.g. methodology, methods, question, epistemology) all coming together to form a cohesive picture. Unlike the rigidity of quantitative analysis, one of the exciting aspects of qualitative analysis is that there is no singular, best way to go about it (Campbell et al., 2013). Finding the most meaningful approach to data coding and analysis will be determined by the research questions, type of study, available resources (including any time constraints) and researcher's positionality (Belotto, 2018).

Types of Data

Research data is the information gathered or created to support the claims of your research. It's the proof behind published research findings, whether it's data generated using specific research methods to collate information and experiences or gathered from existing secondary sources. In addition to the raw data, research data includes details on the means used to generate data or replicate results, such as methods, participant sampling and recruitment, research design and analytical framework. Research data can take many forms. In social sciences research, these tend to include:

- documents which may include things like policy documents, court reports, minutes, memos, organisational reports, clinical notes, process recordings
- literature (both peer reviewed and grey), manuscripts, newspapers, pamphlets and magazines
- field notebooks, diaries, journals, laboratory notebooks, observations
- clinical records of treatments and test results
- questionnaires, transcripts, codebooks
- survey responses
- audiotapes, videotapes, vlogs
- photographs, films, digital prints, music
- art, images, storyboards, posters
- slides, artefacts, specimens, physical samples
- collections of digital outputs
- database contents (video, audio, text, images)
- models, algorithms, scripts (more used in quantitative data)
- standard operating procedures and protocols

It is important that data is properly stored and managed (National Health and Medical Research Council, 2018) to ensure ethical integrity, safety and the confidentiality of participants. This includes correctly storing hard and soft copies in appropriate storage locations and using passwords, encryption or other security mechanisms. Most universities and organisations will have a set of data management guidelines that researchers will be expected to maintain and abide by during the data collection process. Many ethics committees will also require information about data storage and management prior to approving any research to be undertaken. These are important ethical questions to think through, particularly if a person has given a blood or saliva sample (e.g. to test for certain health conditions), because questions about who then owns this sample once it has been provided for research have sparked debate among medical, anthropological and social science researchers (Marvasti & Treviño, 2020)

Types of Coding

Data analysis deals with words, language, symbols and their meanings. When you analyse data, you are applying your analytical lens in order to interpret the words expressed by research participants. This is deductive in that you are applying your analytical framework in order to generate meaning (Braun & Clarke, 2006). This is one reason it is important to be up-front in your research design about your epistemology, positionality and theoretical framework. It makes clear from the beginning the way in which you view the world and, thus, how you will be interpreting the data to generate findings. The first step is to organise your data into what is known in research as 'codes'. These codes can be open or selective. In grounded theory research, which is inductive (that is, you try to generate a theory *from* the data rather than apply one *on* the data), you may also draw on axial coding as you refine your data categories (Corbin & Strauss, 2015).

Open

Open coding is generally the first step when you're analysing qualitative research, especially when drawing from grounded theory (Delve & Limpaecher, 2022). Imagine you've gathered data from interviews and transcribed these interviews into written notes. With open coding, you break down that data, that is, the written transcripts, into parts and give them labels, which are called 'codes'. The name 'open coding' suggests that it helps you explore new ideas as you dive into your data (Linneberg & Korsgaard, 2019).

In Vivo

In vivo coding is a technique used in the open coding phase of data analysis. This method captures participants' lived experiences and perspectives by using their exact words or phrases as codes. In vivo codes are verbatim representations (direct quotes) that are used to preserve the authenticity and richness of participants' expressions (Delve & Limpaecher, 2022). This approach contributes to the development of categories and themes during the broader open coding process. Depending on whether you are applying grounded theory methodology, you may then move on to axial coding or, more generally, a second round of coding.

Axial

Axial coding is used specifically when drawing from grounded theory methodology. It is the second step in the overall process of coding qualitative data, following open coding. In contrast to open coding, in which data is broken into discrete parts, axial coding involves establishing connections between codes. These categories act as the 'axes' around which supporting codes revolve (Corbin & Strauss, 2015) The goal is to explore the relationships among different concepts and categories to develop a more structured and comprehensive understanding of the data.

Selective Coding

If you are using grounded theory methodology, selective coding is the final stage of the coding process. It is where you connect all your categories together around one core category in an attempt to define one unified theory around your research (Delve & Limpaecher, 2022). When conducting a grounded theory study, the goal is to achieve a comprehensive understanding of the data and create an explanatory theory, and open axial and selective coding are often used to achieve this (Corbin & Strauss, 2015).

Descriptive Coding

With Descriptive coding, you summarise the content of the text into a description. The code name should be a word or a noun that encapsulates the contents of the qualitative data. It is a common and simple yet effective way to code qualitative data (Wæraas, 2022). Unlike more interpretive coding methods, descriptive coding aims to provide a straightforward account of the data without introducing extensive interpretation or theoretical framing. It helps us to organise and condense large amounts of qualitative information into manageable and meaningful categories, contributing to a clear and systematic understanding of the data (Saldaña, 2021).

Attribute Coding

As the name suggests, attribute coding involves categorising data based on specific attributes or characteristics. This method focuses on identifying and labelling particular traits, qualities or features within the data. For example, in the analysis of interview transcripts, attribute coding might involve labelling responses according to specific traits or virtues expressed by participants. This approach helps researchers organise and understand the data by highlighting key characteristics relevant to the research question or objectives (Linneberg & Korsgaard, 2019).

Values Coding

With values coding, you code excerpts that pertain to the participant's values, attitudes and beliefs. Values coding helps reveal the participants' perspectives, attitudes and moral considerations, providing insights into the underlying principles that influence their experiences or behaviours (Hedlund-de Witt, 2013). This coding method focuses on capturing the implicit or explicit values present in the data, allowing researchers to analyse and understand the ethical, cultural or normative aspects embedded in the information. For this reason, an understanding of the cultural landscape as well as awareness of the researcher's own values is vital to ensuring an authentic representation and understanding of the data.

Using a Top-Down or Bottom-Up Approach to Coding

Qualitative coding is a systematic process that involves categorising excerpts within your qualitative data to uncover underlying themes and patterns. This method is particularly useful for organising unstructured or semi-structured data, such as transcripts from indepth interviews or focus groups, into coherent themes and patterns for analysis (Linneberg & Korsgaard, 2019). By coding your qualitative data, you introduce a level of systematic rigour to your analysis, promoting transparency and reflexivity for both yourself and others involved in the research. This approach not only enhances the reliability of your findings but also allows for a more in-depth exploration of insights that authentically represent the human stories embedded in the data (Charmaz, 2014). Coding in itself is an early form of analysis "in such a way that the 'final' conclusions can be drawn and verified" (Miles & Huberman, 1994, p. 11).

The coding process usually commences with an initial round aimed at summarising or describing excerpts, followed by subsequent rounds that incorporate the researcher's interpretive perspective. Although there is no singular, definitive method for qualitative coding, it is important to ensure your approach supports your research aims. While grounded theory methodology tends to follow an established coding pattern (open, axial, selective), qualitative analysis in general will involve an initial round or phase of coding, and this will then continue until the researcher feels that no new ideas or concepts are being uncovered (Saldana, 2009). Various coding types, presented in what follows, can be employed and adjusted to suit your own research project needs.

Deductive Coding

In deductive coding, a researcher starts with predetermined categories or concepts based on existing theories or literature and applies them to the data. This is considered top-down coding and analysis (Delve & Limpaecher, 2022). For example, in a study examining social isolation among young people, deductive coding might involve categorising interview responses into predetermined themes like 'loneliness', 'friendship' and 'connection'. These predetermined themes or categories are generally derived from established theories or concepts that relate to social isolation, which are often identified and described during the literature review stage of the research project. When you are reading and analysing the transcripts, you may identify particular quotes or phrases that align with these key themes. You will then code the quote or section of transcript accordingly by labelling it with the relevant category.

Inductive Coding

Inductive coding is a bottom-up method in which you generate codes directly from the data. Without predefined expectations, this approach lets the narrative or theory emerge organically from the raw data. It is particularly useful for exploratory research or when aiming to develop new theories, ideas or concepts (Saldana, 2009). An example of inductive coding could involve analysing qualitative interview data about people's experiences with a new community program. Rather than applying predefined categories, the researcher might identify emerging themes and patterns directly from the participants' responses, leading to the development of new codes or categories that capture the nuances of their experiences (Corbin & Strauss, 2015). In practical terms, it is highly likely that you will draw on a range of deductive and inductive approaches to coding as you become immersed in the data (Walter, 2019). If you are interested in inductive coding or grounded theory in particular, a list of useful resources is provided at the end of the chapter under the heading Further Reading.

The Coding Process

Although approaches to coding and data analysis in qualitative research can be fast, it may be helpful to picture the coding as a two-step process (Linneberg & Korsgaard,

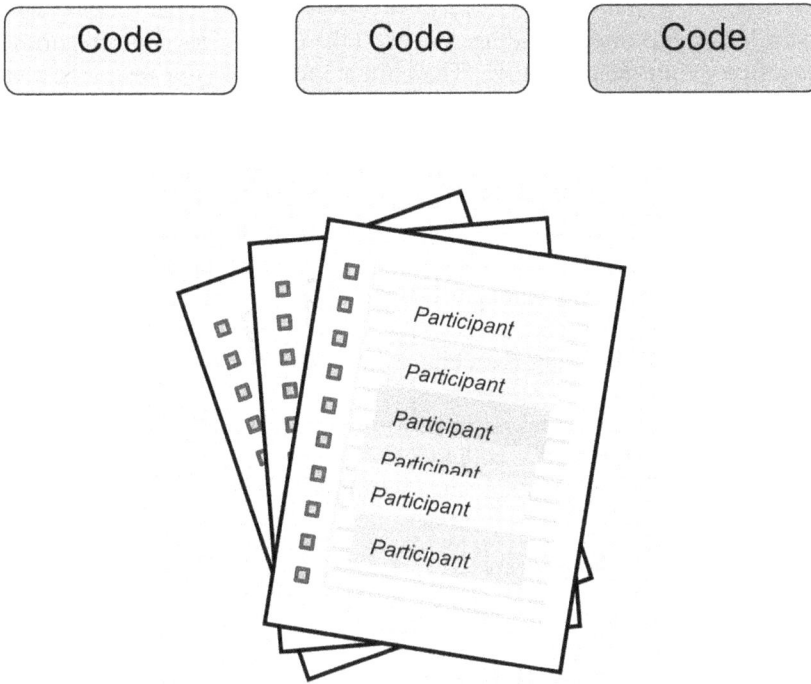

Figure 8.1 Deductive coding

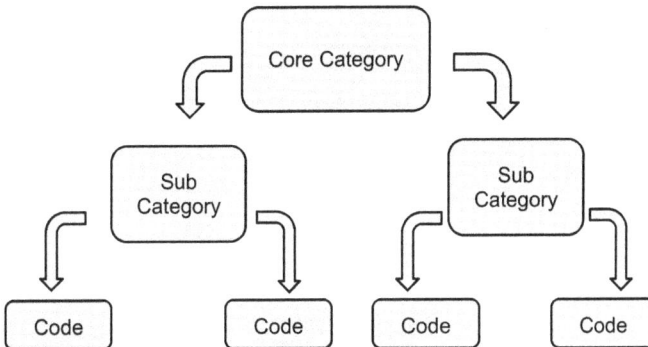

Figure 8.2 Inductive coding

2019). In the first cycle, you focus on terms used by the people you're studying. This is often a more inductive approach (Gioia et al., 2013). In the second cycle (and often subsequent cycles), it becomes more about the researcher, as you bring in concepts and ideas from existing theories to analyse things on a higher level. By breaking down and labelling the data into segments (codes), you can begin to compare similar concepts or ideas people are expressing by gathering all the bits of data that have the same label or code (Linneberg & Korsgaard, 2019). In a similar vein, you can begin to compare and contrast different pieces of data, such as quotes to help uncover differences and divergent views within the data.

After various rounds of data coding, you can take those codes and categories and use them to construct your final narrative. The ultimate result of your research, whether it's a theory, a set of findings or a narrative, can vary based on your research goals. This phase involves merging the creative process of structuring a narrative with the analytical task of linking your narrative to codes and theories rooted in qualitative data (Delve & Limpaecher, 2022). Depending on the amount of data collected, this process can take considerable time. It is important not to try and rush this phase of the research and give yourself time to think, reflect and process information (Anastas & MacDonald, 2000).

Summarising the steps in the coding process:

1 Do your first round of coding the data, which may be based on either inductive or deductive factors.
2 Organise your qualitative codes into categories and subcodes.
3 Do further rounds of qualitative coding.
4 Turn codes and categories into your final narrative.

Narrowing Down the Coding Process

From Coding to Analysis

Coding and interpretation are closely connected processes that evolve together, although they have distinct characteristics. The initial coding cycle involves applying labels to data segments in a somewhat procedural and mechanical way. However, interpreting these codes and deriving an overall understanding is not mechanical – it requires insight to

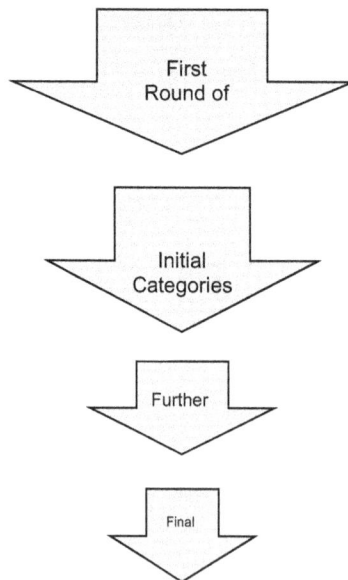

Figure 8.3 Narrowing down the coding process

identify emerging patterns (Linneberg & Korsgaard, 2019). Although software tools can greatly assist with the categorisation, labelling and organising of ideas, they cannot do the thinking for you! In fact, research texts such as this have been criticised for focusing on a procedural, coding-focused approach to data analysis! Critiques say that such an approach serves only to make qualitative methodologies more appealing to positivist or hard-science traditions that require standardised, objective mechanisms (St. Pierre & Jackson, 2014). We recognise this limitation and present an approach to data analysis in this format for teaching rather than for any efforts to ascribe to positivist values or quasi experimental efforts. We acknowledge, particularly in the example of spoken or written text, the power of language in its construction and generation of ideas (as articulated by Foucault). Ultimately, qualitative data analysis is an imperfect process undertaken by imperfect humans attempting to understand an imperfect world. It is the way in which we recognise, acknowledge and grapple with these imperfections and the influence they have on how we see the world that leads to authentic, reflexive and ethical data analysis.

As social workers, we don't shy away from uncertainty, and we encourage you to embrace the process when it comes to data analysis. Lean into what Patti Lather (1991, p. 149) refers to as "the blackhole of qualitative research". This is done through a process of immersion (Walter, 2019). This is where you spend time reading, contemplating, reflecting, revising and essentially in deep thought. Even though the initial research questions can adapt and be refined throughout the coding and analysis process, especially in inductive approaches (Charmaz, 2014), reconciling the chosen question(s) with the raw data is necessary to obtain the answer(s) (Linneberg & Korsgaard, 2019). In many perspectives on qualitative research, the primary aim is theory-building rather than theory testing (Gioia et al., 2013). This means that qualitative research should lead to, for example, the identification of new ways of practice, elaboration of new concepts, theories or ideas, discussions about how different concepts, knowledges and ways of practice may (or may not) relate to one another or accounts of processes or outcomes (Linneberg & Korsgaard, 2019). In the case of social work research, we argue that these findings should ultimately contribute towards the goal of positive social change. While coding is a useful process to help us organise and engage with data, it is our application of theory and awareness of positionality (and, arguably, lack of awareness) to interpret the data which informs our analysis. The process of data analysis is the practical embodiment of linking theory to practise.

Using Computer Software in Qualitative Research

Computer software plays a pivotal role in both the coding and analysis phases of qualitative research data. During the coding process, software provides researchers with efficient tools to organise and categorise large volumes of qualitative data, such as interview transcripts, open-ended survey responses or field notes. These tools facilitate the identification of patterns, themes and relationships within the data, streamlining the coding process and enhancing the researcher's ability to manage complex information (Walter, 2019). Although computer software is not a replacement for human thinking, at least, not at this stage, it can aid the researcher in managing large amounts of data and helping to identify key patterns and themes in the data.

In social science research, one of the most commonly used computer software programs is NVivo. This is used to code, group, label, categorise and store the raw data (e.g. interview transcripts) and to explore the relationships between the coded categories. This is particularly useful when completing a thematic analysis and/or developing grounded theory (Walter, 2019). There is also a range of computer-assisted technologies such as word processing, artificial intelligence programs such as ChatGPT, code-and-retrieve packages such as Ethnograph and a range of new and exciting online tools being created as technology in this space advances. Although social work has historically been sceptical of the use of information technology (Afrouz & Crisp, 2021), other disciplines have embraced the functionality and convenience of computer and data software. While computers and artificial intelligence can serve to aid human research projects, this does not mean that the researcher can hope for the software to do the research for them! The researcher still needs to become immersed in the research data in order to effectively interpret the computer information as well as have the know-how to use the software and technology appropriately. Ethical rigour and principles of social justice, data sovereignty and integrity are just as relevant and applicable when using software to assist the research process as they would be in any other stage of the research process.

Conclusion

Coding and analysis, integral processes in social research, possess distinctive characteristics yet evolve together. The initial coding cycle involves mechanically labelling data segments, while the subsequent interpretation of codes requires insight to discern emerging patterns. Although critics argue that a procedural, coding-centric approach in qualitative methodologies caters to positivist traditions, emphasising standardised, objective mechanisms, our aim in this chapter is to support the reader by presenting ideas in a straightforward, step-by-step way. We are also of the view that although software tools can facilitate coding and organisation, they fall short of replacing critical thinking. We recognise that qualitative data analysis is a subjective, often imperfect process, and acknowledging the power of language in constructing ideas, particularly in spoken or written text, is crucial. In light of the fluidity of qualitative data analysis and the social justice imperative of social work research, a willingness to be reflexive is a key element of the analytical process. This means the researcher maintains a critical awareness of their position, power and influence in the study design, participant recruitment, data collection and data analysis.

Further Reading

Charmaz, K. (2014). *Constructing grounded theory*. Sage.

Miles, M. B., Huberman, A. M., & Saldana, J. (2013). *Qualitative data analysis: A methods sourcebook (Incorporated)*. SAGE Publications.

Saldaña, J. (2015). *The coding manual for qualitative researchers*. Sage.

Strauss, A., & Corbin, J. (1990). *The basics of qualitative research*. Sage.

Walter, M. (2019). Chapter 13: Analysing qualitative data. In *Social research methods* (4th ed.). Oxford University Press.

References

Afrouz, R., & Crisp, B. R. (2021). Online education in social work, effectiveness, benefits, and challenges: A scoping review. *Australian Social Work*, 74(1), 55–67. https://doi.org/10.1080/03 12407X.2020.1808030

Anastas, J., & MacDonald, M. L. (2000). *Research design for social work and the human services*. Columbia University Press.

Belotto, M. J. (2018). Data analysis methods for qualitative research: Managing the challenges of coding, interrater reliability, and thematic analysis. *The Qualitative Report*, *23*(11).

Braun V., & Clarke V. (2006). Using thematic analysis in psychology. *Qualitative Research in Psychology*, *3*(2), 77–101. https://doi.org/10.1191/1478088706qp063oa

Campbell, J. L., Quincy, C., Osserman, J., & Pedersen, O. K. (2013). Coding in-depth semistructured interviews: Problems of unitization and intercoder reliability and agreement. *Sociological Methods & Research*, *42*(3), 294–320. https://doi.org/10.1177/0049124113500475

Corbin, J., & Strauss, A. (2015). *Basics of qualitative research, techniques and procedures for developing grounded theory* (4th ed.). Sage.

Delve, Ho, L., & Limpaecher, A. (2022). How to do open, axial, & selective coding in grounded theory. *Practical Guide to Grounded Theory*. https://delvetool.com/blog/openaxialselective

Gioia, D. A., Corley, K. G., & Hamilton, A. L. (2013). Seeking qualitative rigor in inductive research: Notes on the Gioia methodology. *Organizational Research Methods*, *16*(1), 15–31. https://doi.org/10.1177/1094428112452151

Hedlund-de Witt, N. (2013). An overview and guide to qualitative data analysis for integral researchers. *Integral Research Center*, *1*(75), 76–97.

Lather, P. (1991). *Getting smart: Feminist research and pedagogy with/in the postmodern*. Routledge.

Linneberg, M. S., & Korsgaard, S. (2019). Coding qualitative data: A synthesis guiding the novice. *Qualitative Research Journal*, *19*(3), 259–270.

Marvasti A., & Treviño, A. J. (2020). *Researching social problems*. Routledge.

Miles, M. B., & Huberman, M. A. (1994). *Qualitative data analysis* (2nd ed.). Sage.

National Health and Medical Research Council. (2018). *Australian code for the responsible conduct of research*. Australian Research Council and Universities Australia, Commonwealth of Australia.

Saldana, J. (2009). *The coding manual for qualitative researchers*. Sage.

Saldaña, J. (2021). Coding techniques for quantitative and mixed data. *The Routledge Reviewer's Guide to Mixed Methods Analysis*, 151–160.

St. Pierre, E. A., & Jackson, A. Y. (2014). Qualitative data analysis after coding. *Qualitative Inquiry*, *20*(6), 715–719. https://doi.org/10.1177/1077800414532435

Wæraas, A. (2022). Thematic analysis: Making values emerge from texts. In *Researching values: Methodological approaches for understanding values work in organisations and leadership* (pp. 153–170). Springer International Publishing.

Walter, M. (2019). Chapter 13: Analysing qualitative data. In *Social research methods* (4th ed.). Oxford University Press.

9 Findings, Theory and Agency

Chapter Summary

- Research findings emerge after data analysis.
- The commitment to social justice is central to the identification of research findings.
- Social researchers have a responsibility to understand research findings in their historical, social, political and cultural contexts.
- Understanding both participant agency and social structure is central to social research findings.
- Researchers must position participant experiences within a strengths-based framework.

Introduction

This chapter discusses the important step social researchers must take between data analysis and the dissemination of research findings. It is during this process that the social researcher will consider the theoretical implications for their findings. This chapter explores the contexts in which this process takes place. We begin by considering the 'so what?' question before moving on to explore the positioning of our research findings by considering agency and structure. The chapter concludes with a reminder that the researcher ought to be aware to whom the research belongs.

The 'So What' Question

In Chapter 8, we presented the ways in which data are analysed in a manner that is somewhat procedural in that findings are developed through the analysis of data to develop themes. The next step for social researchers is to ask the 'so what?' question. Say you have undertaken a study to better understand the role that technology plays in the lives of young people in rural settings in Australia. For your methods, you undertake interviews, which are facilitated through the use of visual methods. You ask participants to draw a picture or diagram which represents technology in their lives, and you hold unstructured interviews with them to understand their experience of the phenomena of technology in their day to day lives. You interview 15 people and analyse the data. Bearing in mind the material we have covered in previous chapters, your research can be briefly conceptualised in the following way:

Research question

What role does technology play in the lives of young people aged 12 to 16 years in rural Australia?

DOI: 10.4324/9781003316732-9

Epistemology

Social constructionism

Methodology

Phenomenology

Methods

Interviews, creative methods (visual representations)

Data analysis

Coding for themes

Finding

Young people utilise technology for communication, a sense of community and connection to others.

In making sense of the overall finding, looking for a theoretical explanation is the next step for the social researcher. This may involve acknowledging the limitations of a particular theory and therefore using it in part or adapting it to better account for the findings of the study. The following prompts can be helpful when finding a theoretical explanation for the findings of a study:

• What theory or theories help to explain the findings?
• What do existing theoretical contributions say about the findings?
• What are the main theoretical traditions which have been used in the area?
• What are the tensions between theories in the area?
• Where do the findings 'fit' in relation to the theoretical traditions?

In relation to our example, the researcher will find many contrasting theoretical contributions to the area of technology and social life in contemporary society, and these traditions overlap and oppose one another (Selwyn, 2012). The task of the researcher in seeking a theoretical explanation for their findings is to start with the data and the findings and seek out a theory that explains the findings.

Many researchers and students dread the 'so what?' question because it is when the scholarly work commences. Unlike quantitative or positivistic research, qualitative research seeks to find a theoretical explanation for the findings. This can take a long time and can involve the researcher going back to their literature review, consulting new literature to explain social phenomena and thinking more broadly about the contribution their study makes to the literature.

At the same time, we ought to bear in mind those points made in Chapter 4, where we considered the ethical responsibilities of the researcher. Here, we agree that:

the research process itself has the potential to perpetuate privilege, the status quo, and marginalization of some populations and problems, or . . . it can sensitively and transparently manage the power issues that emerge and instead empower and give voice to vulnerable populations.

(Bentley et al., 2019, p. 434)

Although the terminology of 'vulnerable populations' is used here, we believe that a better term is perhaps 'unrepresented or silenced voices'. The ways in which we represent the views, experiences and opinions of the people with whom we research (participants) must also adhere to our values and commitment to social justice. In Denzin's words, "the heart of the matter turns on issues surrounding the politics and ethics of evidence, and the value of qualitative work in addressing matters of equity and social justice" (Denzin, 2018, p. 19). In this sense, we would see 'vulnerable' subjects as having their own agency and processes of resistance in the face of injustices. The term 'vulnerable people' should therefore be understood as being framed through processes we know deliberately silence particular groups, for example, colonisation or the patriarchy. Let us now move on to think more about what this might mean for research findings.

Agency and Structure

One of the key debates in the theoretical work of the social sciences is wrestling with the tension between agency and structure (Giddens, 1984). Agency relates to our capacity for free choice, and structure relates to social structures which are "composed of a variety of social institutions, such as the education system, the family, the economic system, the political system, the mass media, the military and the legal system" (Van Krieken, 2017, p. 5). Different theorists within the social sciences, and in particular in sociology, have differing positions about the degree to which individuals have agency given that societies' institutions and structures that limit their choices. In social work scholarship, there is a paucity of overt engagement with this debate; however, there *are* differences in the approaches we use.

All of the theories used in social work which underpin practice for working with individuals, groups and communities will have an underlying assumption about the degree to which individuals can have agency within oppressive social conditions. Social work is unique in this sense: the psychosocial approach recognises individual factors that limit individual choice but also maintains the view that social conditions can and do limit individual agency. Qualitative research "attempts to show how individual troubles and problems become public issues. In the discovery of this nexus, it attempts to bring alive the existentially problematic, often hidden, and private experiences that give meaning to everyday life as it is lived in this moment in history" (Denzin, 2018, pp. 31–32).

In *critical* research, which we promote in this book, research is positioned as being able to have an emancipatory end. This doesn't mean that we can irrevocably change the world for the better (if only!), but it recognises that research has the potential to bring about positive change in some way. Critical approaches not only theorise power relations and the ways that social structures affect individual experiences, but they seek to bring about positive change. Whereas social theories seek to provide a theoretical explanation for a particular phenomenon, critical theories provide a theoretical explanation for a particular phenomenon *and* include an analysis of power *and* consider how to bring about positive social change. In sociology, an awareness of the transformative power that critical theory brings is a:

relatively recent occurrence . . . A 'critical' sociology is one which seeks not just to explain the social world but rather to see what is hidden and, in particular, to highlight the forms of power and inequality which exist. As a result, it will often take the position of the powerless against the powerful. In this sense, it follows on from Becker's idea of the sociology of the underdog but with a wider normative goal. . . [which] . . . aims not just to understand the underdog but to 'emancipate' them.

(Dawson, 2016, p. 21)

In social work, we know that historical harms have been inflicted in the name of 'doing good' (Bennett, 2021), so emancipatory aims need to be carefully considered. Research that occurs within communities, by a researcher who is a member of a particular community, for example, provides an inoculation against misguided emancipatory goals. This is because the aims of the research can be agreed on by the people with whom the research takes place.

In Chapter 3, we explored the framing of research questions and discussed the ways in which research questions can act to further oppress or reproduce inequalities. Similarly, when a researcher comes up with findings from their research, it is important to maintain our values and commitment to social justice. In Chapter 4, we considered the role that the research plays in the co-production of knowledge (Franklin & Franklin, 2021). This is relevant when thinking about the overall findings of a research project and relates to how we represent the voices, stories and experiences of research participants.

To understand data in this way is to locate a phenomenon in its historical, social, political and cultural contexts. If we are researching a community that currently experiences oppression and disadvantage, it is the responsibility of the social researcher to understand how individual experiences of participants are impacted by structural conditions. The following are questions that researchers may find helpful to understanding an overall finding of their data analysis to avoid the reproduction of stereotypes or paternalistic narratives about participants as well as to account for agency and structure:

- Have participants' acts of resistance been appreciated?
- What understanding does the researcher have about issues historically faced by their participants?
- What are the current narratives about the participants in the research literature?
- What resources did participants draw from in their environment?
- What structures, systems or institutions seek to silence participant voices?
- What disciplines have dominated research with this community?
- What are the dominant stories told about this community, and who tells the stories?
- What is the researcher's position or perspective?
- What power does the researcher have access to in relation to the community, institutions, knowledge systems?
- Why does the researcher think the research is important?
- To whom is the research relevant?
- How will participant perspectives be privileged?
- How does the researcher plan to position participant knowledge?

Asking these questions can help to position the research findings in a way that takes into account the struggles that individuals may experience but will also ensure that the researcher doesn't overlook participants' strengths. In social work, a strengths-based approach (Saleebey, 2013) helps social workers to avoid pathologising others. Similarly, narrative therapy is another theory used in social work which starts from the assumption that individuals routinely exercise agency against oppression, even in the face of an enduring 'problem' (Morgan, 2000). The language that researchers use to position individuals within social structures must also reflect a strengths-based approach: the use of the term 'victim/survivor' in domestic and family violence research and scholarship is one example. Denzin argues that the social researcher is "called to change the world, and to change it in ways that resist injustice while celebrating freedom, and full, inclusive participatory democracy" (Denzin, 2018, p. 32). Such a stance recognises that we live in an unequal society, where issues such as poverty, violence, oppression and discrimination based on gender, class, sexuality, dis/ability, culture, race and age affect individual and community experiences. This helps the researcher move away from an individualistic explanation for phenomena while privileging stories of resistance, collective action and community in the face of social oppressions.

To Whom Do the Findings Belong?

Understanding to whom the research belongs is crucial throughout social research. This could be a community of people, people who have lived experience of a particular phenomenon, as well as broader society. The findings of a research project can be communicated in a myriad of ways as we discuss in the proceeding chapter, and the role of the researcher is to communicate research findings to whom the research matters. This also calls into question the position of the researcher in coming up with research findings.

Research design is an important aspect to consider in the planning stage because it can mean that if, for example, a researcher is part of the community in which the research takes place, methods to co-produce research findings can be woven into the research design. This would involve the researcher working with participants to come up with research findings and having a consensus within that community that the findings faithfully connect up the research question and data. This approach is one in which the expertise of the people with whom the research has taken place is recognised and centred throughout the research process.

Conclusion

This chapter has explored the ways that researchers produce research findings after data analysis. We have considered the 'so what?' question as well as the positioning of research findings in relation to what this says about the degree to which people have agency in society. We now move on to explore some of the key ways that researchers communicate research findings through the process of research dissemination.

Further Reading

Bennett, B. (2020). Chapter 3 Acknowledgements in Aboriginal social work research: How to counteract neo-colonial academic complacency. In S. Tascon & J. Ife (Eds.), *Disrupting whiteness in social work* (pp. 91–107). Routledge.

Denzin, N. K. (2018). *The qualitative manifesto: A call to arms*. Routledge.

Mafile'o, T., Mataira, P., & Saxton, K. (2019). Towards a Pacific-indigenous research paradigm for Pacific social work. In J. Ravulo, T. Mafile'o & B. Yeates (Eds.), *Pacific social work* (pp. 209–220). Routledge.

May, T., & Perry, B. (2022). Chapter two: Social theory and social research. In *Social research: Issues, methods and process*. McGraw-Hill Education (UK).

References

Bennett, B. (2021). *Aboriginal fields of practice*. Bloomsbury Academic.

Bentley, K. J., Mancini, M., Jacob, A., & McLeod, D. A. (2019). Teaching social work research through the lens of social justice, human rights, and diversity. *Journal of Social Work Education*, *55*(3), 433–448. https://doi.org/10.1080/10437797.2018.1548985

Dawson, M. (2016). *Social theory for alternative societies*. Palgrave Macmillan.

Denzin, N. K. (2018). *The qualitative manifesto: A call to arms*. Routledge.

Franklin, A., & Franklin, A. (2021). *Co-Creativity and engaged scholarship: Transformative methods in social sustainability research*. Springer Nature.

Giddens, A. (1984). *The constitution of society: Outline of the theory of structuration*. University of California Press.

Morgan, A. (2000). *What is narrative therapy? An easy-to-read introduction*. Dulwich Centre Publications.

Saleebey, D. (2013). *The strengths perspective in social work practice* (6th ed.). Pearson.

Selwyn, N. (2012). Making sense of young people, education and digital technology: The role of sociological theory. *Oxford Review of Education*, *38*(1), 81–96. https://doi.org/10.1080/03054985.2011.577949

Van Krieken, R. (2017). *Sociology* (6th ed.). Pearson Australia.

10 Dissemination, Impact, Engagement and Research Translation

Chapter Summary

- Dissemination is important to the research process because it enables research findings to have broad reaching impacts.
- Understanding where research findings belong involves understanding the purpose and aims of the research.
- Researchers have ethical responsibilities in relation to disseminating research findings.
- Innovations in research dissemination enable research to reach a broad audience.
- The role of the public intellectual is important to research translation.

Introduction

This chapter considers research in its contexts. For example, some research will seek to better evaluate the efficacy of particular programs, and the ways in which the findings will be disseminated will likely be through the agency where it sits. Other research seeks to offer alternative explanations for particular phenomena: how does the social researcher get the findings of the study out there into the broader public eye? This chapter will examine these questions and discuss how dissemination is always dependent upon the research objectives, the research question and the topic of the research. Dissemination is not simply a matter of a set of tasks: careful consideration about where to present research findings is a question which involves social work theory and values (Barnes et al., 2003). In this chapter, we consider these alongside particular attention to newer methods of research dissemination, such as the use of social and other media to translate findings of research into tangible outcomes. Social work theories which argue for an emancipatory outcome for practice will be explored and considered in relation to research and subsequent dissemination.

The chapter will also provide information about ways to contribute to the broader community through the development of particular tools based on the research in question, such as through handbooks, podcasts, vlogs and so on. How to utilise more traditional media is also explored, and tips for working with print, radio and television audiences will be provided.

Dissemination and Impact

Research dissemination relates to the ways in which the findings of a research project are communicated, and 'impact' is a term associated with the ways in which research makes a, sometimes measurable, difference. Imagine you are co-parenting a small child, and you want to know about other parents' experiences of co-parenting. You might feel isolated and

DOI: 10.4324/9781003316732-10

not have many connections to others in a similar situation to you. If you did want to find out about what research might have been done to explore co-parenting experiences, you might do a web search. This search might bring up an academic paper which reports on a research project in which people with co-parenting experience spoke about some of the challenges or strategies they employ to parent a child across two households. From your web search, you might also come across a media piece that features someone who is co-parenting along with a summary of the research. After you read the journal article, you feel less alone because you have read the stories of other parents in a similar situation to you. After you read the media article, you discover that there are online resources that could help you in your parenting. In both of these examples, there is an 'impact' or change which has resulted from accessing this information. Yet how do we measure such an impact from a research point of view? It's almost impossible to measure individual reactions or subtle differences in the way individuals might approach an issue because they have read about a particular piece of research.

Increasingly, funding bodies, universities and organisations undertaking research are interested in making sure that research findings make their way to an intended audience and contribute to positive change. Impact can be *measurable* and help the researcher demonstrate that their research will benefit others. However, for many researchers, 'impact' is a problematic term because "social scientists and publishers of social science all know that impact is a complex, subtle, diffuse and many-layered effect that accumulates through time" (Marar, 2022, p. 821), as we have seen in the example. Before we consider how to measure impact, let's explore how researchers tell others about their research findings.

Particular methods for communicating results will depend on to whom the research is of interest. The choice of dissemination methods ought to be informed by the perspectives of participants and stakeholders, such as advocacy groups, who would have a stance on who needs to know about the findings of the research (Rawsthorne, 2024). Thinking about who needs to know about the research is therefore connected to how this is best communicated. A lot of dissemination strategies rely on written forms of communication (Tisdall, 2009), even though there is a myriad of ways that researchers can creatively communicate research findings to an intended audience. Like all other stages in the research process, ethical issues ought to be considered alongside decisions about dissemination.

Ethical Issues

Deciding how research findings are communicated involves going back to the research question and the aims of the research. Questions of ethics are always bound to such considerations because of the ways in which the researcher will need to grapple with the question: to whom does this research belong? Here, ethical principles used in social work can help. These are often outlined in national statements about research (Gambrill, 2016, p. 79) and relate to a researcher's ethical responsibilities. Social work values along with biomedical ethics have similarities to research ethics. Here, we consider some of the fundamental virtues associated with social work more generally and note the importance of these elements to research dissemination.

Beneficence and Non-Maleficence

Beneficence and non-maleficence relates to doing 'good' and avoiding harm. Though it seems a fairly obvious maxim that "social workers should not harm their clients" (Reamer, 2013, p. 33), we know that social workers have caused harm under the guise of what they perceive to be 'doing good' (see, for example, Bennett, 2021).

In terms of dissemination, 'doing good' and avoiding harm relate to the way in which we talk about our research. Being respectful to participant stories, faithfully reporting on our findings and acknowledging the tone in which we report our findings are important. If we think about some key social work principles such as social justice and a commitment to human rights (Hölscher et al., 2023), the stories that we tell about our participants through dissemination methods need to uphold the principles to which social work is committed.

We argue that doing 'good' ought to be balanced against the principle of respect (see Beauchamp & Childress, 2020). Respect for autonomy and a strengths-based lens ensure that we avoid pathologising participants, recognise the social inequalities that shape individual experience (Dunk-West & Verity, 2013) and protect us from paternalistic or superficial research findings conveyed through dissemination.

Veracity

Veracity means telling the truth. In social work practice, being honest is crucial to the people with whom we work: from service users/clients to colleagues and supervisors (see Banks, 2021). In terms of research dissemination, telling the truth about research findings is the obvious connection to veracity, but it can also mean being honest about the limits to the research in question. In qualitative research, we can only speak on behalf of the findings of a small group of people, so when we disseminate our findings, being transparent about the findings and overall contribution of the study to broader scholarship is central to our commitment to veracity in relation to dissemination.

Fidelity

Fidelity means taking seriously the professional promises we make (Reamer, 2013). In social work practice, this involves being able to fulfil the promises that we make with clients: if we say we are going to do something, then it is important that we uphold the standards of the profession by delivering those things that we promise. In relation to research dissemination, fidelity relates to the promises we have made to our participants about where the research will be communicated. If we say, from the outset of our study, that we will write a report or present the findings to the broader community and we tell that to our participants, we ought to fulfil that promise.

Confidentiality

Confidentiality is a principle well known to social workers in which we ask people to trust us with their private details. In terms of research, keeping participant anonymity is something considered in the ways in which we report research. In dissemination activities, it is important to make sure we are protecting the identities of our participants by removing identifying details, being aware of information that might make it easy to identify someone. This is particularly the case for people in small communities. For example, if a researcher is reporting on a small study in a regional area with a particular community, when they publish from their findings, they may need to consider whether that community is identifiable. The onus here on the researcher is to be able to faithfully represent data from the study in a way that protects confidentiality. Another issue related to confidentiality and dissemination is to ensure that people participating in the research are aware of where the information they provide will end up. This, again, highlights the need for researchers to formulate a research dissemination strategy at the planning stage, because participants' consent includes the use of their data.

Other questions which can help researchers make decisions about research dissemination include:

- Who needs to know about the findings of the research?
- Are the research findings easy to understand?
- What messages about the findings need to be conveyed?
- Is there a public interest in this research?
- Do the research findings contradict with current accepted wisdom about the topic?
- What future needs are identified in the research?
- What social policies are relevant to the research?
- How does the research contribute to existing scholarship about the topic?

Let's now think about some potential options for sharing research findings. The following table offers some suggestions about potential dissemination methods, noting who needs to know and how we communicate research findings to this particular audience.

Broad research focus	Who? Group or community to whom research is being disseminated	How? Activities or communication methods	Reason for dissemination type
Examining healthy relationships for young people	Young people	• Posters with infographics • Social media platforms utilising short videos • Publish the research in a peer-reviewed journal article • Conference presentation to teachers	• Increase awareness about healthy relationships • Prevent young people experiencing domestic and family violence (DFV) • Tell other researchers and academics about the research findings

Measuring Impact and Publishing Options

As discussed, measuring impact is not without its challenges and ought to be understood through a critical lens; however, there is another way to think about impact through asking: What would the point be of research if its findings only stayed with the researcher? Traditional research dissemination often occurs through publication in an academic journal. Peer-reviewed journals are those in which an original research article will be sent off to experts in the field of study who scrutinise the article for omissions and accuracy as well as assess the arguments made in the article for their robustness and utilisation of existing knowledge. The evolution of journals in an age of metrics has meant that journals are often ranked in order of prestige, and researchers located in universities will often be encouraged to only publish in what they regard as high-quality journals (Gruber, 2014). Notwithstanding the difficulties in navigating the world of rankings, including which journal in which to publish, journal articles continue to be an effective way to disseminate research findings. One way to measure the reach of a published article in a peer-reviewed journal is to look at how many other researchers have cited the article; however, caution should be used when using only this as a measure of research quality, given that some research areas are under-researched and under-theorised, and therefore, only a smaller percentage of researchers will be interested in citing the research. For the purposes of thinking about dissemination, it is helpful to understand that citation metrics are readily available to researchers and are one way to measure impact, albeit with some caveats (see, for example, Haddow & Hammarfelt, 2019).

Some research projects seek to better understand the efficacy of particular programs or policies, and as a result of the research, subsequent changes to practice or policy may eventuate, and these are examples of research impact. In terms of the research dissemination for these kinds of research projects, they may take the form of a research report.

Research report formats differ depending on the discipline and purpose of the report (Osiochrú, 2022). Generally speaking, research reports will commence with an introduction and will detail the research methods, findings and a conclusion. Executive summaries are also useful at the beginning of a report and summarise all of the points made in the full report, including the research findings and conclusions.

If the research project has enough depth to warrant writing a book, thinking about the audience is again important. The audience for a trade publication is the general public, whereas a research monograph will be of interest to an academic audience. Most major publishers will have information about how to submit a book proposal on their websites, and commissioning editors' details will be listed. Commissioning editors are the first point of contact to see if there might be an appetite for a particular book idea.

Research Translation

Many social work journals will need social research findings spelled out for their social work audience. This is, in our view, one of the problems with social work literature: there is a kind of anti-intellectualism pervasive to the discipline, which means that it is not enough for the social work researcher to simply be curious about individuals, groups and societies and to seek knowledge and insights into human behaviour. It is in this context that research involving insights into human behaviour or societal characteristics is not specific enough to be seen as relevant to social work. Instead, many social work journals want their articles to report on research and *translate* the findings for a social work practitioner audience. Just as with the issues explored earlier in the chapter associated with research metrics, the move towards always having a measurable outcome relating to research is part of a broader neoliberal shift in which knowledge for its own sake is underappreciated unless it has measurable implications. Here, it is not enough that research findings are interesting or reveal new insights into human behaviour or changing trends, for example. In the wake of this anti-intellectualism in social work, authors Singh and Cowden argue that social workers ought to see themselves as 'transformative intellectuals' (Singh & Cowden, 2009). In this context, there are many positive possibilities for researchers. We think that social workers who undertake research ought to be seen as having much to contribute to developing ideas about society, communities and individuals. Research translation therefore becomes about speaking from an empirically informed knowledge base to facilitate 'knowledge mobilisation' (Aiello et al., 2021). Translation can occur with many end users. With organisations, this might involve the researcher providing an overview of their research findings with suggestions about how the findings might be incorporated into practice or policy.

Research translation with the media positions the public intellectual as a spokesperson for research-derived insights. The researcher as the public intellectual will be interested in conveying research findings to a lay audience. Here, a researcher with expertise will be able to provide commentary that relates in some way to their own research or body of scholarship. For example, a researcher who has undertaken empirical work with parents and undertaken projects relating to caregiving, education and child protection and has a background in working in practice with children, young people and their caregivers, will have drawn conclusions about what the key issues are facing caregivers and parents. A journalist may be preparing a story exploring the challenges facing parents in modern life and may be seeking the expertise of a researcher in this area. The journalist will want some expert commentary that can speak confidently about this topic. Here, research translation will involve a researcher being able to synthesise all that they have learned from their practice and research and be able to articulate to a lay audience some of the key messages.

Creative and Emerging Dissemination Methods

Creative methods for communicating research findings are often connected to the methods used in data collection. Photo elicitation or other ways of representing identity will produce visual artefacts which can be displayed through an art exhibition to a particular community (see, for example, Toone, 2023, p. 78). Increased use of social media platforms opens up new opportunities for researchers to display, promote and discuss their research findings. These include, as noted, both traditional media and newer media such as podcasts, blogs and vlogs.

Conclusion

This chapter has argued that dissemination is a process that must be congruent with the values inherent to social work involving understanding dissemination in its context, both in the institutional setting, such as within the academy, as well as the context in which the research topic is located. To this end, we have explored the contemporary ways that research is measured and evaluated for its impact. We have also explored some of the complexities involved in this research landscape. Dissemination is therefore something that needs to be planned and justified at the research proposal stage. We have also argued that it is a researcher's ethical responsibility to amplify the voices of our participants. Sharing one's personal experience with a researcher can be an onerous activity, and we ought to carry the responsibility of having oversight of a range of people's experiences with a sense of duty. Emerging technologies and media practices, alongside traditional dissemination practices, offer the researcher novel ways to amplify the voices of our participants.

Further Reading

Barnes, V., Clouder, D. L., Pritchard, J., Hughes, C., & Purkis, J. (2003). Deconstructing dissemination: Dissemination as qualitative research. *Qualitative research: QR, 3*(2), 147–164.
Clark, T., & Bryman, A. (2019). *How to do your social research project or dissertation.* Oxford University Press.

Dawson, L. (2023). Chapter 6: Beyond box ticking and buzz words: A queer, working-class, Anti-racist, anti-ableist sharing in UK Academia. In Y. Taylor, M. Brim & C. Mahn (Eds.), *Queer precarities in and out of higher education: Challenging institutional structures*. Bloomsbury Publishing.

References

Aiello, E., Donovan, C., Duque, E., Fabrizio, S., Flecha, R., Holm, P., Molina, S., Oliver, E., & Reale, E. (2021). Effective strategies that enhance the social impact of social sciences and humanities research. *Evidence & Policy*, 17(1), 131–146. https://doi.org/10.1332/1744264 20X15834126054137

Banks, S. (2021). *Ethics and values in social work* (5th ed.). Red Globe Press.

Barnes, V., Clouder, D. L., Pritchard, J., Hughes, C., & Purkis, J. (2003). Deconstructing dissemination: Dissemination as qualitative research. *Qualitative Research: QR*, 3(2), 147–164. https://doi.org/10.1177/14687941030032001

Beauchamp, T. L., & Childress, J. F. (2020). Response to commentaries. *The Journal of Medicine and Philosophy*, 45(4–5), 560–579. https://doi.org/10.1093/jmp/jhaa011

Bennett, B. (2021). *Aboriginal fields of practice*. Bloomsbury Academic.

Dunk-West, P., & Verity, F. (2013). *Sociological social work*. Ashgate.

Gambrill, E. D. (2016). *Social work ethics*. Routledge. https://doi.org/10.4324/9781315242842

Gruber, T. (2014). Academic sell-out: How an obsession with metrics and rankings is damaging academia. *Journal of Marketing for Higher Education*, 24(2), 165–177. https://doi.org/10.1080/08841241.2014.970248

Haddow, G., & Hammarfelt, B. (2019). Quality, impact, and quantification: Indicators and metrics use by social scientists. *Journal of the Association for Information Science and Technology*, 70(1), 16–26. https://doi.org/10.1002/asi.24097

Hölscher, D., Hugman, R., & McAuliffe, D. (2023). *Social work theory and ethics ideas in practice* (1st ed.). Springer Nature. https://doi.org/10.1007/978-981-19-1015-9

Marar, Z. (2022). On measuring social science impact. *Organization Studies*, 43(5), 821–824. https://doi.org/10.1177/01708406221086703

Osiochrú, C. (2022). *A student guide to writing research reports, papers, theses and dissertations*. Routledge.

Rawsthorne, M. (2024). *Using social research for social justice: An introduction for social work and human services*. Routledge.

Reamer, F. G. (2013). *Social work values and ethics* (4th ed.). Columbia University Press.

Singh, G., & Cowden, S. (2009). The social worker as intellectual. *European Journal of Social Work*, 12, 479–493. https://doi.org/10.1080/13691450902840689

Tisdall, E. K. M. (2009). *Researching with children and young people: Research design, methods and analysis*. SAGE Publications Ltd.

Toone, K. (2023). *Straight for pay. Lesbian and queer sex workers: Understanding the effect of capital on identity and community*. Flinders University, College of Education, Psychology and Social Work.

11 Conclusions

Chapter Summary

- In this chapter, we remind readers that social research is a political process, driven by ideological forces, worldviews and discourse.
- This chapter reflects on the key ideas presented in this book by summarising the chapters.
- Social work research should drive a social justice agenda and seek to contribute to positive social change.
- Social work research must be responsive to social issues, conditions and movements and expand its reach beyond the narrow perimeters of fields of practice.

Introduction

This chapter provides a summary of previous chapters and a discussion of social work research and the use of research in the future of social work practice across a range of settings. We show that social workers are uniquely positioned to drive ethical social research that aligns with a vision for a more socially just world. We re-assert the values-laden nature of social research and reject the premise that research can ever be neutral, unbiased or objective. Such a belief is often used to maintain an inherently white, Western epistemological agenda and devalues the experiences, beliefs and voices of First Nations and other marginalised communities. We round out this chapter by considering research evolution into the future and the role that we, as active consumers and producers of research, can play in this process.

Social Research for Social Change

In beginning this book, we drew from the work of Seidman to highlight the aspirations of early practitioners who aimed to bring about positive change in the world. We align ourselves with the belief that social and critical theory act as a conduit to achieve these goals, contributing to positive social change in complex, contemporary times (Seidman, 2016). In this vein, we position social research within a critical framework that seeks to further amplify social work's commitment to social justice and human emancipation (Morley et al., 2019). We argue that any social research conducted by social workers should drive positive change, fostering shifts in understanding and amplifying the voices of those historically silenced. Engaging in research involves constructing knowledge and contributing to the understanding of a particular social phenomenon or experience. We strongly

DOI: 10.4324/9781003316732-11

emphasise the ideological pitfalls of dominant discourse and research bias, particularly in marginalising diverse knowledges, including that of First Nations communities. By grasping the processes of knowledge construction and consumption, we can critically examine the voices and opinions that may hold privilege in the research process. This awareness allows us to be mindful of our research position and appreciate the importance of critical reflection in social work research, aiding in navigating epistemological tensions.

Research projects are inherently political because they involve actively constructing knowledge and uphold a process of determining what types, and whose knowledge is considered valid and important. This book has consistently advocated for social work researchers to be mindful of the complex forces influencing knowledge and research practices. We have emphasised the roles of critical reflection, reflexivity, positionality and drawing from a social justice lens to debunk research processes that serve to perpetuate the interests of an academic elite rather than reflect the views and narratives of the communities we engage. In unraveling these forces, we have hoped to guide readers in thinking critically about research, aligning with social work values and fostering positive social change.

Reflecting on Our Journey

In Chapter 1, we clarify what is meant by the terms 'social research' and 'social justice' and invite the reader to reflect on what these terms mean to them. Drawing from the work of Leavy (2022), we suggest that social research serves multiple purposes, namely, to explore, explain, evaluate and, ultimately, enact social change. We assert that research is inherently influenced by the researchers themselves, drawing from feminist, decolonising, constructionist and critical research traditions. As such, we provide a statement of our own positionality as a way of outlining our engagement with the key ideas and concepts presented in this book.

In Chapter 2, we explored the social construction of knowledge and discussed this in line with the key research terms 'epistemology', 'ontology' and 'axiology'. We hope that this chapter has helped to demystify some of the language used in social research and can assist in making social research more accessible. We recognise that the use of academic terms, particularly in discussions about research, is often represented by a white, Western standpoint that serves (albeit inadvertently) a neocolonialist agenda. We value and recognise diverse knowledges and ways of engaging, understanding and interpreting the world around us.

Chapter 3 delves into the process of approaching a research area, guiding readers on crafting effective research questions informed by the insights from Chapter 2's discussion of epistemologies. Chapter 4 navigates ethical considerations in social research, emphasising the understanding of personal values and the role that social justice plays in orienting the researcher and the people with whom they research. We then move into a practical guide for approaching and conducting a literature review, as an essential component of ethical and well-informed research, in Chapter 5.

Chapter 6 undercovers a range of methodologies and their application in social research. It highlights the way in which your epistemology, values, research question and consequential research design all converge to form a coherent approach to research that, ideally, supports the social justice mandate of critical social work. We then add to this in Chapter 7 by presenting a range of qualitative research methods that align with constructionist, interpretivist, standpoint and feminist epistemologies. In Chapter 8, we support the reader in approaching data analysis by outlining some of the logistical aspects of data management, coding and approaches to interpretation.

Chapter 9 again asks us to be critically reflexive and to ask ourselves "for whose purpose?" has this research been conducted. We addressed the significance of the 'so what?' question and the placement of research findings concerning what it reveals about individuals' agency in society. Finally, in Chapter 10, we assert that dissemination is a process that must be congruent with the values inherent to social work. The chapter emphasises the ethical responsibility of researchers to plan and justify dissemination at the proposal stage, emphasising the duty to amplify participants' voices through various means, including emerging technologies. Honouring participant voices, acknowledging positionality, maintaining ethical rigour and pursuing positive social justice remain key themes throughout the entirety of the book.

Where to From Here?

We see the crucial role that social work can play in offering a critical approach to social research into the future. Social work ought not be bound by the narrow constraints of fields of practice. What we do with the people with whom we work is far richer than the limits set by organisations, governments and funding bodies. Conversations with the people with whom we work are often rich and creative. They move across individual issues to social issues to political and cultural contexts, ebb and flow across people's identities and behaviours and have us thinking about life in all its challenges and breadth. Research undertaken by social workers needs to acknowledge our sociological imaginations and see that we offer unique and valuable perspectives on the complexities of social life. As we grapple with the effects of climate change, increasing technological advance and life on this planet, we also see the effects of oppression and inequalities and see the ways in which people resist and form collectives and communities that demonstrate strength and power in the face of adversity. We hope for a future in which social workers see critical research perspectives as yet another tool for positive, emancipatory change.

Further Reading

Banks, S. (2021). *Ethics and values in social work* (5th ed.). Red Globe Press.

Crotty, M. (2020). *Foundations of social research: Meaning and perspective in the research process*. Taylor & Francis Group.

Rawsthorne, M. (2024). *Using social research for social justice: An introduction for social work and human services*. Routledge.

Smith, L. T. (2021). *Decolonizing methodologies: Research and indigenous peoples*. Bloomsbury Publishing.

References

Leavy, P. (2022). *Research design: Quantitative, qualitative, mixed methods, arts-based, and community-based participatory research approaches*. Guilford Publication.

Morley, C., Ablett, P., & Macfarlane, S. (2019). *Engaging with social work*. Cambridge University Press.

Seidman, S. (2016). *Contested knowledge social theory today*. John Wiley & Sons, Incorporated.

Index

For Product Safety Concerns and Information please contact our EU
representative GPSR@taylorandfrancis.com
Taylor & Francis Verlag GmbH, Kaufingerstraße 24, 80331 München, Germany